TIWI

THE LIFE AND ART OF
AUSTRALIA'S TIWI PEOPLE

TIWI

THE LIFE AND ART OF AUSTRALIA'S TIWI PEOPLE

HEIDE SMITH

INTRODUCTION BY LIONEL HUDSON

JB GIFTS J.B. GIFTS & BOOKS EDITION HABIT PRESS

This softcover edition is an exclusive joint production by
Edition Habit Press, Sydney and J.B. Gifts & Books, Adelaide, Australia
First published in hardcover by Angus & Robertson, 1990

Written enquiries should be made to the publisher:
Edition Habit Press Pty. Ltd.
112 Bronte Road, Bondi Jct. NSW 2022, Australia
Tel. 02 387 4339 / Fax 02 389 2966
J.B. Gifts & Books
P.O. Box 118 Marleston Business Centre S.A. 5033
Tel. 08 297 1669 / Fax 08 297 1669

National Library of Australia
Cataloguing-in-Publication Data

Smith, Heide
Tiwi, The Life and Art of Australia's Tiwi People

ISBN 1-87616-00-0

An Edition Habit Press Production
Printed in Hong Kong

TO
NGIYA MAMANTA TIWI
(my friends the Tiwi)

ACKNOWLEDGEMENTS

In a way this is a book of the Tiwi people by the Tiwi, for it would not have been possible to produce it without their total commitment and friendly cooperation.

Sister Teresa Ward of the Our Lady of the Sacred Heart Convent, Nguiu, Bathurst Island, is one of the most knowledgeable people on Tiwi culture. She has been of enormous help, and has provided valuable material, some of which formed the basis to the text.

I am also grateful for the help and advice given to me by Brian Smith, Elizabeth Lindsay, Vera Bachinger, Bryce Courtenay, Jill Hickson and Peter Fitzhardinge.

Sponsors for this project were The Tiwi Land Council, Australian Institute for Aboriginal Studies, Kodak (Australasia) and Bron Elektronik (Switzerland).

Encouragement came from Professor Manning Clark and Dymphna Clark and His Excellency the Governor-General of Australia, Bill Hayden.

I especially wish to mention that the Tiwi elders have granted me permission to keep the photographs and names of the deceased in this book, even though they might at some time be Pukumani (taboo) in Tiwi custom. For this I am extremely grateful.

FOREWORD

In Australia a long overdue revolution has begun in the attitude of the white inhabitants of the continent to the original tenants of the Australian wilderness. The early descriptions of the Aborigines by white navigators and explorers were most unfavourable. In the 1620s the Dutch seaman who landed on the shores of northern Australia described it as a land of sand, flies and 'black barbarian savages'. The English seaman William Dampier, at the end of that century, described the natives on New Holland as the 'miserablest people in the world' who 'differ but little from brutes'.

Now, at long last, the damage inflicted by such accounts of the Aborigines is being repaired. The white people of Australia are gradually dropping the myth of the Aborigines as 'savages' or people who for some inscrutable reason were condemned to perpetual childhood. The historians and the artists are now putting together a quite different picture of the history, achievements and character of the Aborigine.

The photographer is Heide Smith who is well known for her portrait and landscape studies and is a happy blend of the craftsman and the mature artist. It would be presumptuous of me to comment on her skill. All I can do is urge as many people as possible to view this collection of photographs of Tiwi people in their home on Bathurst and Melville islands. Heide Smith not only has an eye for the beauty and dignity of these people, she understands the simple truth that without their ancestral lands life loses much of its meaning for the Aborigines. They decay, they become a prey to the aberrations and vices of the white man.

This book is a hymn of praise to a people who have survived the ordeal which began with the coming of the white man in 1823.

It is a delight to the eye; it is a source of wisdom to those with eyes to see. It entertains and it instructs. I hope very many people will enjoy it and ponder the message these pictures and their story can convey to us.

Manning Clark

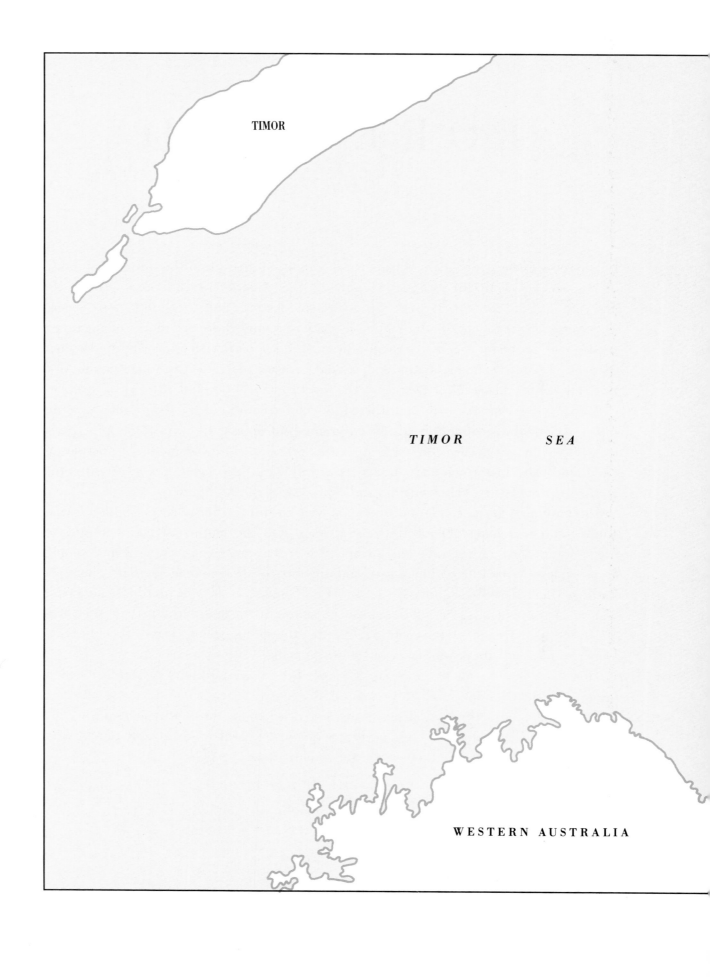

TIMOR

TIMOR   *SEA*

WESTERN AUSTRALIA

BATHURST AND
MELVILLE ISLANDS

Pularumpi
Milikapiti

BATHURST ISLAND

Apsley

Port Hurd

Taracumbe Falls

MELVILLE ISLAND

Strait

Paru

Nguiu

Van Diemen Gulf

Clarence Strait

Beagle Gulf

■ DARWIN

NORTHERN TERRITORY

Mary Dechantel Timaepatua. Wisdom and
innocence blend on a child's face.

INTRODUCTION

The Tiwi people occupy Bathurst and Melville islands in the Arafura Sea, just north of Darwin in the Northern Territory.

Their ancestors had their first contact with Europeans 157 years before Captain Cook landed in Botany Bay. Even today they steadfastly embrace much of their old culture, which is rich in rituals distinctly different from those of the Australian mainland Aborigines. For example, they never threw the curved boomerang. They still gather 'bush tucker' with relish, and their numbers are growing.

There is no argument that the first Tiwi, like the mainland Aborigine, came to Australia by way of the chain of islands to the north-west. With the rise in ocean levels after the last ice age some 10 000 years ago, the Tiwi were isolated from the influence of other humans for thousands of years; even from those across the narrow stretch of water that separated them from the mainland. They remained cut off until relatively recent times.

Today the leaders of the Tiwi are working on projects to increase employment among their people. The majority of Tiwi are on social welfare, or 'sit-down money', but in many cases the Tiwi only get this payment if they participate in community work. As with all emerging people the Tiwi have their problems in today's sophisticated world, but, bolstered by their hardened survival instincts, they have so far coped fairly well with this pressure and are continuing to show resolve to preserve their heritage. 'This is our way,' they say.

Undoubtedly the Tiwi's most valuable assets in this regard are their innovative art forms, their carving and their painting, which have already roused considerable interest in the outside world.

Heide Smith first met the Tiwi people in 1987 while on assignment in Arnhem Land. She had been island hopping in the Arafura Sea aboard a roll-on landing barge called *Trisha Kate*. It is the supply vessel that ploughs between ports on the northern coast of Arnhem Land, around the Crocodile Islands, and to Bathurst and Melville. It delivers essentials like tea, sugar, building materials—even disposable nappies. The barge doesn't take passengers, so Heide became cook for the voyage.

From her first day on the islands she was captivated by the Tiwi and their unique culture; she wanted to get to know them better and she wanted to photograph them.

The *Trisha Kate* calls once every two weeks at
Nguiu, Bathurst Island. Its pre-dawn arrival causes
a buzz of activity in the normally quiet township.

Heide lives and works among the political tribes of Canberra. She calls herself a 'people photographer' and has clients who range from plumbers to prime ministers.

On her return to Canberra she put up the idea to the Tiwi Land Council, the main decision-making body for the two islands, that she produce a collection of photographs of their people for a book and an exhibition.

When the Council accepted the proposal, Heide was both surprised and overjoyed. The Tiwi elders, the Council said, saw the significance of halting time and recording their people for history. Heide was given permission to stay on the islands for as long as she needed to complete her work.

She returned four times to the islands. She lived with the Tiwi in the bush during the dry season and in the settlements of Nguiu, Milikapiti and Pularumpi in the wet season, all in all about five months. During that time she kept a journal of her experiences living the Tiwi way and extracts from it are included here.

Heide restrained her excitement about the official sanction. That was fine, but, as an experienced photojournalist, she was acutely aware that she still needed to be accepted by the people themselves. This was their land and they were suspicious of outsiders. Only a few months before a French woman photographer had been ordered off the islands because she had taken shots of a funeral without permission.

After a week on Bathurst, a flimsy plane dropped Heide off in shimmering heat on the airstrip at Milikapiti, on the shore of Snake Bay, Melville Island. She braced herself to face the formal gathering of tribal elders which would really decide the fate of her project.

––––––

Heide's truck, on loan from the Tiwi Land Council,

served as transport for many Tiwi friends as well

as a vehicle for her equipment.

It is like a dream. I can't believe I'm really here, standing alone before fifty-two seated Tiwi elders who don't look all that friendly. I am not very good at public speaking and now I have to address these Tiwi men who are suspicious of this white woman and her camera.

I feel my face going red—and not just from the heat of the day. Fans are whirring, dogs are barking in the distance, and I pull myself together to make my plea to the Tiwi. I talk about my wish to photograph their people as they really are and not as the tourists want to see them.

I mention ceremonies and funerals and I hear an uneasy grumbling in the audience. 'No funerals,' somebody calls and the others shake their heads in agreement. I try a different approach: 'All right, you tell me whenever I can't take pictures.'

I ask them to tell their families about me and my camera so they won't turn their backs to me when I approach them. 'I am not a tourist or a newspaperman,' I say. 'I am here to stay and go bush with your people. I would like to be their friend if they will accept me.' It is out now. I feel better.

There is a lot of Tiwi talk and I try not to think too much about the outcome. Then I see heads nodding. They are all terribly serious but I am promised cooperation. The ice is broken. The Tiwi elders have accepted me. Their people, I hope, will accept me too.

Barney Tipuamantumirri, a Tiwi elder, in front of
an old hut that he built when he was a young
boy.

In the settlement of Nguiu Heide found a valuable source of information and an enthusiastic supporter in Sister Teresa Ward, in the white veil and habit of the order of Our Lady of the Sacred Heart.

Sister Tess is the daughter of a Victorian farming family. Her given church name is Sister Teresa, but as a Tiwi named Teresa died last year that name is Pukumani, or taboo, on the islands for twelve months.

Sister Tess is the teacher/linguist at St Therese's School, a cluster of red-roofed buildings near the seashore on Bathurst. Many of the concrete walls are painted gaily with Tiwi motifs. She arrived at St Therese's School in 1971 and in four years had set up a bilingual programme there. She was largely responsible for turning the oral Tiwi language into a written one, a significant step towards preserving the culture of the Tiwi people. Sister Tess has made a study of the customs and history of the Tiwi and has been happy to pass on the results of her dedication to Heide.

It was Gerardine Tungatalum who introduced Heide to Tiwi life. Gerardine is a widow in her sixties. Tall, with graceful movements, she is a leader among women. She does not chatter, yet she is a wonderful storyteller. She does not shout, yet everybody listens to her and takes notice. Her husband, some twenty-five years older than she (as is often the case with Tiwi marriages), died of snakebite. Like most Tiwi women, Gerardine walks barefooted, wears a skirt and top printed and sewn in the island's workshop, and wears no jewellery or adornments.

For Heide, her chance introduction to Gerardine was one of those rare moments of instant understanding. She felt she had known this total stranger from a strange culture and a different world all her life. During her stay on the islands Gerardine was like her shadow, something she could not be without. Often this 'shadow' played a leading role in negotiations.

Gerardine calls Heide 'ngipuka'—my sister.

Sister Tess with Tiwi teachers at the school on Bathurst. Left to right: Magdalene Kerinaiua, Ancilla Puruntatameri and Marguerita Kerinaiua.

Gerardine is ready to go. She is standing next to her place with a bag over her shoulder. She is wide awake, scrubbed clean, her hair still wet—a contrast to the others around the camp all rolled up in blankets near the dead fireplace. The dogs are still sleeping too until they hear my truck approaching. Their greeting is a snarl. Gerardine climbs aboard and before the night quite fades away we are on our way to Tarantipi to catch crabs.

The truck, on loan from the Land Council, runs well. My new friend knows the turn-offs. After an hour on various dirt tracks we arrive at the open sea.

The sun comes up suddenly, painting the world around us. Now it is hot, the glare from the white sand hurts my eyes and my bare feet burn.

We walk across the beach to the muddy creek entrance, where we poke around with sticks to find the crabs. As a grandmother, Gerardine does a lot of child minding but hunting is her passion. Our catch piles up. She knows just where to find the crabs. She shows me how to pull them out of the mud without being nipped by the snapping claws. Gerardine moves further up the creek, and I shout to bring her back: 'No further. Not for me.' Gerardine looks about her. 'You right, croc might be coming.'

Back out of danger on the open, white beach we collect pretty shells.

At low tide in the mangroves that surround the islands the ground is alive with mudskippers, crabs and millions of red sandflies.

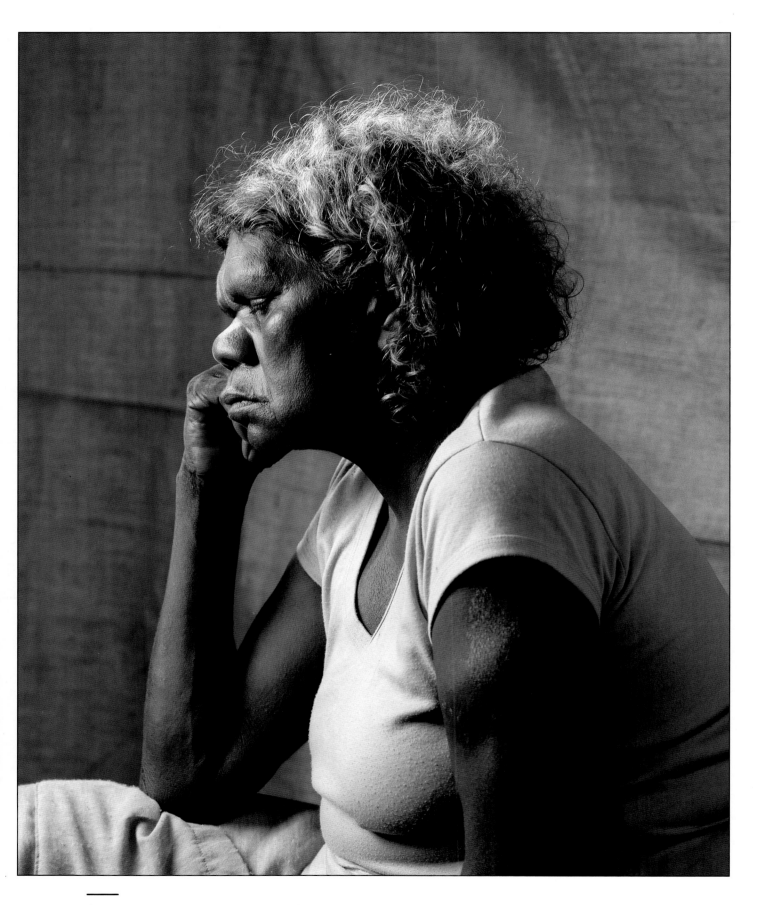

Gerardine Tungatalum, Heide's 'sister'.

It was the first of many hunting trips with the Tiwi for Heide. She slept in the bush with them and ate bush tucker.

The Tiwi keep out of the sun where possible and this suited Heide down to the ground. She mostly photographed them in the shade of shelters or trees, away from the glare, to capture the detail and texture of their dark faces. On black and white film she over-exposed and under-processed by one stop.

There were few language problems. Some people had fair English and Heide had a smattering of Tiwi, which contains a lot of sign language anyway.

Her rapport with Gerardine was special. They became close friends. It was Gerardine who smoothed the way in the villages and who helped to break down the suspicions of the old people.

The white flaky flesh of the copper snake is quite delicious.

Suddenly I am wide awake. Something is wrong. The bush is strangely silent. No noises.
What's happened to the cicadas, the frogs, the night birds? I strain my ears and pick up only the distant thunder of the breakers on the beach. There is no moon, no stars to relieve the blackness. There's something in the air. A cold shiver ripples over my body. Then I hear voices, first sleepy, now urgent, fast chatter from the other side of the camp: 'Yirrikipayi . . . yirrikipayi . . . [crocodile . . . crocodile].'

Our camp on the edge of the Arafura Sea stirs into action. Fires are rekindled, babies silenced at their mothers' breasts and the men stagger into the night armed with clubs, knives and guns.

Scared and excited, I reach for my flashgun. So far my shots of salt-water crocodiles have been with a long lens from a boat and even that, at the time, seemed quite risky. But no close-ups tonight. The men come back with reports of skid marks in the sand halfway around the camp, but no crocodile. It must have been spooked by the flickering fires and the commotion and has slipped silently back into the sea.

I can't sleep. The mournful cry of the curlew drifts through the night. It must be near morning now. My face, hair and blankets are wet with dew. I get up to stamp life and warmth back into my stiff limbs. Carefully, I step over my sleeping friends on my way to find firewood. Their bodies are cocooned in grey blankets—not only to keep out the cold but also unwanted visitors like copper snakes and scorpions.

Firewood is scarce close to the camp so I need to fossick further out. By the time I return Sarah has the fire going. She is blowing at the flames, extending her long, graceful hands towards the fire. 'Good morning, mantanga [friend],' she says.

Gerardine arrives at the fire with a billy of water from a nearby stream. We talk about the night and the crocodile. Gerardine snorts: 'He big humbug!' I'm puzzled. 'Who, the croc?' Gerardine pokes the fire angrily. 'No, that man who shouted about the croc. He always makes much of nothing.' 'But a big croc is not nothing,' I argue. Gerardine leans forward to check whether the water is boiling. 'It would have gone away anyway, no need to wake the whole camp.'

Sarah is silent. She's busy retrieving the leftovers from last night's dinner. They were in a billy hung in a tree to keep them away from the dingoes. What about the green ants, I wonder. Perhaps they are vegetarians. I am passed a piece of grilled flying fox but I insist somebody else has it. I am a creature of habit and prefer to make do with my own dried fruits, nuts, muesli and coffee.

Left: Campsite at Port Hurd with its sentinel.

Right: Palm nuts are a natural remedy for worms and were staple diet not so long ago.

On Bathurst and Melville annual rainfall can exceed 1000 mm a year, which is double the amount, for instance, that Sydney gets. The trouble is that these torrential rains fall mostly in the months of December, January, February and March, flooding vast areas of low-lying country. This is the Wet. Cross-country travel is difficult and hunting game restricted. As they have done for thousands of years, however, the Tiwi resign themselves to what they call Jamutakari and adjust their lives accordingly.

Most of the tribal groups moved out of the hinterland after the Second World War, lured to the community centres in Nguiu, Pularumpi and Milikapiti by the stores, the schools, the workshops, the churches and the clubs. Although these people now live on the outskirts of civilisation the mournful cry of the stone curlews just before dawn is still their wake-up call and in many households old folk still greet the morning with songs of grief in memory of someone who has just died.

Children join the family around the cooking fire for a cup of strong, black tea. If they are lucky there may be some turtle or wallaby meat leftovers from the previous evening. Otherwise, many go off to school on a piece of damper.

The school bell beckons at 8 a.m. and children running late race off as bright and as well-brushed as children anywhere at the beginning of the day.

Mostly the weather is fine in the mornings so the traditional hunting and foraging goes on for what the Tiwi consider 'real food'. They crave bush tucker to supplement the food they buy from the store. In the first light women without paying jobs go out digging bush potatoes and gathering berries, while the men hunt wallaby or go to sea to harpoon turtles. The Wet is the best time of the year to catch green turtle and to gather their eggs from nests on the beaches.

At a school celebration. The Tiwi elders teach the children ceremonial dancing as well as face and body painting.

With the rains come the green tree frogs in their teeming thousands. They turn up everywhere: in the kitchen sinks, the wash tubs and the toilets. Heide tells a story of one leaping out of a dress she was pulling over her head in her bedroom.

The croaking chorus from the frog fraternities comes in waves and seems to add to the serenity of the scene once the school quietens down for the morning. Card players gather in the shade of mango trees. They play a game called 'thirty-one' and the news and gossip of the day is swapped between deals.

Other groups sit around singing songs and telling stories. It is this oral tradition that has kept the Tiwi culture alive. All the talk is in Tiwi. These people are more comfortable conversing in their own language although they learn to read and write at school in both English and Tiwi. It was at the literary centre of St Therese's School, Nguiu, that Sister Tess and helpers put the oral Tiwi language into writing. Mary Godfrey, from the Summer School of Linguistics, who has lived on the island for many years, has the task of teaching all Tiwi who are interested to write in their own language.

Traditional dancing with its chanting accompaniment is taught in the schools by Tiwi elders anxious about the survival of their culture.

The Catholic Mission runs the schools on Bathurst but the schools and adult education centres on Melville are public schools with white Australian teachers.

The angry monsoon clouds build up during the day and then at three o'clock, almost without fail, the rain thunders down. It brings relief from the burning heat and also delights the children because it provides miniature lakes everywhere for them to sail their makeshift boats.

There are about equal numbers of white and Tiwi teachers.

At last, the dry season, time for many Tiwi to go bush and live as their ancestors did. They can't wait to get out of the cyclone-proof houses that they use during the Wet. Each extended family goes off to its own hunting ground, or homeland. The village is deserted. All they take with them in the way of food is flour, sugar and tea. Their meals come from the bush or the sea.

Some growing-up kids take along their transistor radios. Gerardine disapproves of this. 'He must watch out for those snakes. They like music and will come to that thing.'

Most people make their own music. They sing a lot. At night a big fire is made on the beach and the little ones join in the ritual dances around the flames.

Each family has its own dreaming dance, inherited from the father's side. Those not performing shout and stamp and keep the rhythm with clapsticks. All eyes are on the steps of the dancers. This is serious business for the young boys. The girls are laughing. All you see of them in the light of the flames are their shining eyes and rows of white teeth.

The Dry is the happy season. The sea is mostly calm. The men go to sea in small aluminium dinghies, which have replaced dugout canoes, to spear turtle, barramundi and salmon; also to harpoon snakes and sometimes dugong.

Alfonso, Edwina, Marie Evelyn, Stanley (the Mission names don't seem to fit this scene) and I are off to another island to collect crabs. My camera gear is stowed away in a watertight container. I sit in the bow, my legs dangling over the edge. I close my eyes to enjoy the refreshing spray of sea water over my face. This is heaven until Stanley tells me in no uncertain terms to pull my legs in if I don't want to lose them to a shark or crocodile.

I quickly save my legs from that fate but I can't do much about my burning skin until we reach the island. Then I dress for the heat. My head is wrapped in an old scarf, a T-shirt covers my braised shoulders and I put blockout cream on my face. It's hardly fair. My friends don't have to bother with any of this.

On the sand my feet burned so I put on thongs. Now we are in the mangrove swamp I have them in my hand. The mud is knee deep in parts. Only the anticipated taste of crab meat in my mouth keeps me going.

We reach a horror stretch of tangled roots and slimy mud. Stanley waves us back. 'We go there, not here. This no good.' Some of the others start to object but give in when they realise he has chosen an easier route on my account. He did not want me to feel inadequate.

The Tiwi are sensitive people, communicating more with motions and signs than with words. And they invariably think and act for everyone in the group, not just for themselves. I wonder whether there is even a word in their language for 'me' or for 'I'. The word Tiwi means: we, the people.

Tiwi boys with the bare essentials needed for a
bush camp.

For thousands of years the Tiwi, we are told, believed that their two islands composed the entire world of living people. Their Dreamtime, their culture, flowed from this belief.

Some say the term Tiwi means 'we, the only people', which is in line with that thinking. However, if it had never crossed the minds of the early Tiwi that there might be other human beings on earth why would they have needed to lay claim to being the only ones? Could it be that Tiwi means simply 'us' or 'human beings' as distinct from the other living creatures—the fish, the birds and the animals?

Noted anthropologists have been trying to solve the Tiwi riddle for eighty years or more but no-one claims to have the answer. Scholars of Australia's human prehistory agree that the Tiwi and the Australian Aborigine are descended from the same early humans, the Australoids, who drifted in waves to the northern shores by way of a chain of islands from the Asian land mass, which then included Java. That was over the period from 7000 to 40 000 years ago, plus or minus a few thousand. Whatever the exact date the Tiwi settled their islands, there followed a long period when they developed their own culture in isolation.

The stretch of water that separates Melville Island from the Australian mainland narrows down to thirty-eight kilometres at one point. Without doubt the Tiwi would have known that there was land there. Even in the early days when their only water craft were made from bark and were not terribly seaworthy, they would have seen the lightning-sparked bushfires in the distance.

But to the Tiwi of the 'time before', their word for the past, the smoke of the mainland fires signified a spirit world, a place where their souls went after death. Over there was the home of the dead.

The earliest recorded Tiwi contact with Europeans dates back to 1623 when the Dutch circled the islands. Then followed raids by Portuguese slave-traders from Timor. They were interested only in the women, who probably ended up in the slave markets of Batavia (Jakarta) and Macao. Bartering with ships that stopped for water and to salvage pieces of iron off wrecks introduced the Tiwi to the iron age.

By the late eighteenth century the Macassans from Celebes and the Malays came in their sail-rigged, dugout canoes, looking to replenish their fresh water on their way to gather trepang—sea slugs—in the shallow waters off northern Australia. There was fighting on the beaches and the Tiwi warriors seized prized axes and the odd canoe. With handy timber on their islands and now axes to work with they promptly copied the canoe design and this opened up their world. They now had seaworthy craft that enabled them to make occasional raids on the nearby mainland to capture young Aboriginal girls. Their weapons were spears and ironwood throwing sticks. These had a knob at one end and were nothing like the mainland boomerang.

The Tiwi craving for the wondrous creation, the axe, landed them in trouble when the British started worrying about the security of the vulnerable north-west of their new colony.

In 1818, Norfolk Island-born Lieutenant Phillip Parker King, son of the early governor of New South Wales, surveyed the islands and named Melville after Viscount Melville, head of the Admiralty, and Bathurst after England's Colonial Secretary of the time.

Then in 1824 three British ships, filled with soldiers and convicts, turned up to build Fort Dundas on Melville Island. This was the first white settlement in northern Australia and a British reaction to the increasing activities of the Dutch East India Company. After five years of strife, caused mainly by Tiwi spear attacks on the British with the idea of stealing their axes, and also by the outbreak of disease, the fort was abandoned.

A present-day Tiwi writer ends his account of this period with: 'Even today many Tiwi still wonder why the British came and stayed in a place that did not belong to them anyway.'

Nobody had informed the Tiwi, but by 1825 the boundary of New South Wales had been pushed to the 129th parallel and all Aborigines had been relieved of their rights to traditional tribal territories. For the Tiwi, life went on pretty much as usual, although it wasn't until 1976 that the Tiwi were granted inalienable freehold title to their islands, which means that the land cannot be sold or mortgaged.

In 1911 Father Francois Xavier Gsell, a young Alsatian priest, set up a Roman Catholic Mission on Bathurst Island. By 1920 there was a school at the Mission at which all classes as well as the church services were conducted in the Tiwi language.

Bathurst and Melville have been called the 'Sentinel Islands' because they are at the gateway to northern Australia for travellers from South-East Asia. They lived up to this name on the morning of 19 February 1942. Six Japanese Zero fighters peeled away from the bombers they were escorting to a raid on Darwin and strafed the church and a DC-3 transport plane on a nearby landing strip on Bathurst Island. These were the very first enemy bullets ever to bite Australian soil. One Tiwi man was wounded in the leg. There was no doubt that the pilots would have been fully briefed about the two islands because the crews of Japanese pearling luggers knew them intimately.

The moment the Japanese planes were sighted overhead Father John McGrath radioed an air-raid warning to naval headquarters in Darwin but, apparently, no action was taken there. Just twenty-four minutes later Japanese bombs started to rain down on a surprised Darwin.

Later one of the Zeros, which had been hit by anti-aircraft fire over Darwin, crash-landed on Melville Island. A Tiwi named Matthias Ulungura stalked the pilot, who was armed with a revolver and a knife, and grabbed him from behind.

'He got proper big fright,' Matthias said afterwards. 'I take revolver from his right side near his knee. Then I walk backwards pointing gun. I say "Stick 'em up, right up . . . two hands . . . no more holding hands on head".' With help from some other Tiwi he took away the captured pilot's clothes and boots and handed him over in his underpants to the RAAF on Bathurst.

So it was a Tiwi who captured the first prisoner of war on Australian soil.

North I go towards the equator and to Pularumpi (Garden Point) at the north-west corner of Melville, close to where the British established their settlement back in 1824.

By truck we bump our way across the wide expanse of this sparsely inhabited island. Greener than Bathurst. So remote.

Melville has at least 5000 water buffalo. The British introduced them 160 years ago. They are thriving. The Tiwi hunt them for meat but are making little impression on their numbers.

I have not seen any horses yet but I can smell them. There are 10000 on the island, many of them Timorese ponies. Originally domestic, these animals have been living in the wild for a hundred years or more and are very shy. The Tiwi don't hunt the horses.

My home for the next few days will be the priest's house, the only two-storey timber building on the island. Decay takes over quickly in the tropics. The green ants, spiders, possums, frogs, lizards and the birds—even owls—seem to regard this residence as their own. I throw the switch for the ceiling fans, causing a dust storm. Thank goodness the fridge works and there is an old jug I can mend, so there will be blessed coffee. I find clean sheets in a cupboard . . . amazing. I walk through the village and along the seafront. The heat and the humidity is beating me. I drag myself to bed in the priest's house.

I wake out of a deep sleep within the hour at the croaking of a frog. It must be big and also close but I can't see it. Anyway, I must get up, I have work to do. Today is Sunday and most people are still out hunting and fishing.

I go back to the beach and photograph children there and also a sugar glider changing branches in a flowering gum. I am close but hear no sound. A sea eagle is cruising overhead and the boys copy him, running along the beach with arms spread out like wings.

Joanna Tungatalum from Pularumpi.

Floating in the water are logs in abundance, all looking like crocodiles. No real ones, but you keep looking.

The sun is nearly touching the horizon out there among the islands of Indonesia but the heat is still intense. How I would love to run into the sea and cool off but there are the crocs and the box jellyfish—last year two boys died here from stinger attacks.

I wait until the sun dips into the sea, setting the sky ablaze. In fading light I go home to the presbytery; to the house with many rooms I share with the frogs, the possums and the boobook owl.

In the first light the kookaburras and the plovers wake me. I walk to the sea again and then on to the village where I meet the police tracker, the shopkeeper, the baker and the teacher. 'Good morning mantanga.' I am their friend.

Then there is Joanna Tungatalum, a colourful old character with yellow hair, Frances Borgia Tipakalipa and his wife, Mercy, who has long white hair yet is still beautiful. In the afternoon I have coffee with Mark Lindhberg, the Adult Education and Art Officer, and Cyril Rioli tells me about the pearl farming project of the Tiwi Land Council and their plans to domesticate the buffalo.

At 3 p.m. it rains, right on schedule. The paths turn to creeks. The children love it and so do the frogs.

I photograph Colombiere Tipungwuti, the dancer, practising various animal sequences on the edge of the sea. When the sun starts to set I hint that I don't mind being alone. He says he should stay to watch for crocodiles I might not see. He finally goes when supper calls. I feel good being alone here watching the sun spectacular at the edge of the Tiwi world.

Cyril Rioli, Deputy Chairman of the Tiwi Land Council.

Father Gsell's reluctant 'flock' were, to a white person's way of thinking, naked primitives. They lived off the land, they were able to survive without outside help and they lived in a Dreamtime world of spirits.

For a number of years after the missionary joined them, frail and disabled people were still being buried alive when the Tiwi considered they were 'close up finish'. Unwanted children, especially twins, were dealt with the Tiwi way. That was tribal business. There was blood-drinking from each other regardless of whether either person was suffering from leprosy, yaws, tuberculosis, hookworm or fever.

Then, even more of a problem in the eyes of the Mission, there was a form of racial suicide, in that young men were not able to marry. This was a flow-on from the Tiwi's age-old custom of polygamy. A man's prestige was measured by the number of his wives, who were his food-gathering unit.

Fathers promised their daughters at birth to other old men in what was little more than a business deal. They were handed over at puberty, but there was no such thing as a marriage ceremony. They had always 'belonged' to their husband.

It was all to do with the Tiwi idea of where babies came from. The Tiwi, along with other Australian Aborigines, generally did not believe that the male had any role in human conception. It was their belief that a woman became pregnant as a result of a spirit entering her body. The Tiwi, however, went a step further than the mainlanders in dealing with the unpredictability of the spirits.

Anthropologists C. W. M. Hart and Arnold R. Pilling explain it this way in their book, *The Tiwi of North Australia*:

'Because any female was liable to be impregnated by a spirit at any time, the sensible step was to insist that every female have a husband all the time, so that, if she did become pregnant, that child would have a father.

'As a result of this logical thinking, all female Tiwi babies were betrothed before or as soon as they were born; females were thus the 'wives' of their betrothed husbands from the moment of birth onward.

'For similar reasons, widows were required to remarry at the gravesides of their late husbands, and this rule applied to even feeble great-grandmothers who had already buried several husbands in the course of a long life.

'It can readily be seen that these rules—prenatal betrothal of female infants and immediate remarriage of all widows—effectively eliminated all possibility of an unmarried mother or a fatherless child. No matter where the unpredictable spirit chose to create the baby, whether it was in the body of a pretty young woman, a toothless older one or a youthful teenager, the female would have a husband and the children when born would have a father.

'The Tiwis were thus probably the only society in the world with an illegitimacy rate of zero.'

Of course, the husband of the pregnant woman was not always the father of the baby girl but he still had the power of betrothal. This was quite an asset and he invariably made a point of investing it to his own advantage.

The end result was that only a section of the males in the tribe finished up with wives. Of course, the shrewd dealers among them had more than their share. Even sixty years ago an old man with twenty to twenty-five wives was not exceptional. They tell of the father of a Tiwi named Finger who had twenty-nine wives. Mainland Aborigines did not take polygamy to this extreme.

It is not surprising, therefore, that these young bloods without any prospect of getting a wife were regarded with suspicion by the older generation. Women could only move about in the bush with the permission of their husbands who usually went with them anyhow. The 'big man' needed three or four old widows in his retinue to help him keep a check on his younger wives while they were out hunting and gathering. Despite their surveillance, accusations of illicit sex were still the main cause of discord around the fires at night.

So the young French missionary had to face the perhaps unique situation of a society that had no concept of an unmarried female in its ideology. There was not even a word in the Tiwi language to describe this situation.

Father Gsell was quick to realise there was no point in trying to convert or drastically change the behaviour of the mature Tiwi. His target was the younger generation.

So how did Father Gsell go to the aid of Tiwi men who had reached the age of forty without getting a wife except, perhaps, an elderly widow? Well, he moved into the marriage business.

His first move was to get involved in the rescue of a ten-year-old girl named Martina from the Maola tribe on Bathust Island. She was promised to Merapanui, described as a 'hairy old man with leprosy'. The priest sent her back to the tribe when she ran away the first time but she returned five days later with a spear wound in her leg. When the warriors turned up at the Mission ready for battle Father Gsell had an inspiration. Out came the flour, knives, mirrors, tobacco and a tomahawk. Merapanui was seduced. He sold Martina to the missionary. In no time more young girls were on the market.

Left: Mena Pilakui enjoying a mug of coffee. Like many of the older people, Mena has never known her date of birth and her age is a mystery. Right: Mena Puantulura.

Father Gsell wanted his 'wives' to be free to choose husbands in their own age group as long as they were also eligible within the limits of Tiwi blood relationship laws.

Martina eventually married a young Tiwi named Argus. He was a good husband and a kind father. They had three boys and two girls.

Before long there was competition in the market place. Japanese pearling luggers started making Melville Island an essential port of call, ostensibly for fresh water, but it was clear that they had 'girling' on their minds as well as pearling. The Japanese had loads of trade goods and could offer a better deal to the multi-married Tiwis than could Father Gsell. The pearlers paid for temporary use of the young wives while the Mission wanted their souls permanently.

Father Gsell, who was later to become the first bishop of the Northern Territory, still managed to pile up a score of 150 wives.

Brother John Pye, MSC, in his book, *The Tiwi Islands*, says the last great pagan leader among the Tiwi was a man named Summit who died around 1970. He had a dozen wives and was the last to have more than two.

Summit died a Christian and his final words were that there was to be no 'Pukumani', the Tiwi mourning ceremony, for him. If there was, he said, he would come back and haunt them.

Brother Pye, who still lives on Bathurst Island, says the end of polygamy among the Tiwi has been a factor in breaking down fighting on the islands, especially among the women.

Brother John Pye.

The air is smoky. The Tiwi have been burning off, so it is a good time for hunting. Some women ask me to come along. 'Hunting what?' I ask. 'Oh, most things, like yilinga [copper snake], possum, bandicoot, wallaby and maybe find sugarbag [honey].' I am told to put on shoes. The bush may still be hot from the burning. Also, the fire could have stirred up the snakes. I do as I'm told. 'But what about you?' I ask, looking down at their bare black feet with the white soles. They laugh. 'We don't like wearing shoes— no need.'

About ten kilometres out of Nguiu we stop and leave our truck. We walk miles through the bush, the Tiwi women armed with buckets and axes. I am armed with cameras, as usual. The five of us spread out, calling out now and again to keep in touch.

First I follow Valma, a younger woman. We walk around looking up into the scorched trees, seeking possums which might be leaving their smoked-out homes. Now Valma is interested in an old tree on the ground. She sticks a narrow twig into a hole in the bark. 'Ah . . . sugarbag.' She starts hacking away at the tree with her axe to get at the honeycomb.

I catch up with Gerardine who is catching the sun's rays with the lid of a billy can. I give her my 'what's-going-on?' look. She beckons me to come closer and then I see she is using the tin lid to reflect light into tree stumps. 'Snakes,' she mouths.

Then Gerardine points ahead, 'Dingo . . . something in its mouth. Ah, he's dropped it. Come, see.' The poor dingo is robbed of its catch. We have a wallaby to take home. This will bring a few laughs back in the village.

Later I ask, 'You women do the hunting and most other things. Is there anything only men do?' Gerardine grins, 'Oh yes, they do a lot of thinking.'

Heide's hunting companions with their prize. The women didn't have to kill the wallaby, a dingo did their work for them.

The population of the two Tiwi islands sixty years ago was a shade over 1000. Today it is double that. The Tiwi groups have always spoken the same language, as far as is known, and have followed identical customs.

In fact, these islanders in the Arafura Sea are one of the few Australian Aboriginal tribes still in possession of a native habitat they could live off in the old style if the need arose.

In the course of their age-long cultural isolation the Tiwi have developed a complex kinship system.

Tiwi territory is divided into thirteen 'countries' to which each Tiwi belongs, according to where his or her father belongs. The names of the countries are: Malawu, Minkuwu, Wurankuwu, Jikilarruwu, Murnupi, Wulirankuwu, Jamulampi, Mantiyupi, Arankijarri, Yimpinari, Jurrupi, Yangarntuwu and Marruwawu. Tiwi take their name from their father's homeland. Someone from Jikilarruwu, for example, would carry the name Jikilawila. Children are given their tribal names by their father or relatives on the father's side. A child's first lessons in speech deal with his or her relationship to other family groups. This kinship system is of great importance to the Tiwi. For instance, it is an insult to address someone by name. The kin term must be used if the person is related; if not, they are called 'friend'.

A Tiwi's personal Dreaming dance also emanates from the father. If the father is crocodile (yirrikipayi), then all his children have the crocodile dance too. A Tiwi's Dreaming dance could be a mullet, a woollybutt flower, a white cockatoo, bloodwood or bamboo—whatever their original paternal ancestor turned into when he died.

However, the skin totem system in Tiwi culture is matrilineal and this has a vital

All one family. The Munkara women with their
one 'man', Ambrose, in the front row.

influence on the way of life. The system has four main groups, namely Wantarringiwi, Mantirikuwi, Marntimapila and Takaringuwi, and each of these has numerous sub-groups. The skin totem determines the marriage line. Marriages are arranged between families, but only along the appropriate marriage lines. For example, a person in the Wantarringiwi group can only marry people from the Mantirikuwi or Takaringuwi. They can never marry people from the Marntimapila group.

Complicated though this system may seem, it was essential to an isolated people as a way to avoid inbreeding.

Until the influence of the white man started to change things some fifty years ago, the Tiwi had some strict family laws as well:

When a girl joined her husband after puberty she had to stay close to his parents and relatives and have nothing to do with her own family. At the same time, her husband had to continue to hunt for her parents to pay off the debt he owed them.

A son-in-law was forbidden to talk to his mother-in-law. His wife did the talking for him if he wanted to know anything from her mother. It should be remembered that a man was very often around the same age group as his mother-in-law. To the Tiwi, mothers-in-law were special because from them came the skin group for all the children.

When a brother and sister reached maturity they ceased speaking to each other and were never to be seen together.

Today the Tiwi live closer to the lines of Christian teaching. Old habits die hard, though, and no doubt there are watered-down versions of these family laws still being practised in Tiwi society.

Beatrice and Paul Kerinaiua going bush. Women are still excluded from the Land Council and many are still promised to their husbands at birth, but in everyday life Tiwi women appear to be on equal terms with men.

We are off to see the Portamini people and the Tipuamantumirri people on the west coast of Bathurst Island. I have been told I must take along a guide to deal with the spirits of the land there. (On an earlier trip a Tiwi elder on the back of our truck fired two shotgun blasts into the air to notify the spirits ahead that a non-Tiwi was coming.)

This time I have a special envoy along to introduce me to the spirits. He is an imposing Tiwi elder, Edward Portamini, well over six feet tall with white hair and the traditional white beard.

It took Edward a matter of minutes to pack for a few days in the bush. He strode out of his house with a blanket roll, a coffee mug, a loaf of bread and a roll of toilet paper, tossed them into the back of the truck and said, 'Let's go.' Other Tiwi already out in the bush there will provide us with tucker.

In the Wurankuwu homelands, which is Portamini country, I set up my tripod among tree roots, vines and moss to get shots of some children playing in a clear stream under dense foliage. Suddenly the green ants descend on me. They are everywhere. I feel them in my hair. I clench my teeth and try to ignore them. They won't sting unless I try to squash them. On no, they are in the viewfinder, running wild. I change lenses like lightning. I don't want them inside the camera. I take my pictures before I dare to shake the scurrying devils out of my hair.

Further down the creek a woman does the washing. Her children do the wringing. Under a shelter of branches a young boy is carving a wooden figure under the watchful eye of his teacher, his father.

The Portamini tell us about the feast they had last night—roast wallaby. 'Everyone eat too much. Now resting.'

Now to Rocky Point in Minkuwu homelands. This is Dreaming country, a sacred site, the home of the spirits. It is a point of large grey rocks protruding from the blue sea. We walk towards them with Edward always a hundred metres ahead.

I hear him talking to himself. Then I realise he is calling out to the spirits. He is announcing the arrival of a non-Tiwi to this sacred spot. It must be all right now because he turns to me and beckons. Not too close to the rocks though. Stay here. I am grateful to get this far. It is a memorable sight. The wind and the sea have carved the rocks to the shape of a giant dragon's head.

Later, Edward takes me to meet Barney Tipuamantumirri, another Tiwi elder. This is his country. He proudly takes me around. Only he can permit me to go a little nearer to the rocks, but I'm still not allowed to get close enough for a good shot.

His people are out hunting. The children are looking for ripe pandanus nuts. A dead snake, yilinga, is hanging on a branch near the fireplace; a dead wallaby hangs in a tree, drying out in the sea breeze. It is a very domestic scene. The camp is made under soft, swaying casuarina trees. Their needles carpet the ground below. I can hear the rolling of the sea.

Edward Portamini, painted for a ceremony, near
the old Presbytery on Bathurst Island.

36   Although there was no way they could have known it, the Tiwi have always had a privileged life compared with the lot of their fellow Aborigines on the mainland. Except for one brief five-year encounter they did not have to cope with the European influence until 125 years after the first 'fatal impact' in New South Wales.

More than anything, however, they have always had ample land for their tribe and a plentiful supply of native food.

The ancient Tiwi storytellers would have told you they owe it all to the old blind woman, Murtankala, who arose from the ground carrying three babies in her arms. As she crawled in darkness across the featureless landscape, seawater followed and filled the imprints made by her body. Eventually the pools became one and formed a channel. The old woman continued her journey and once again the moulded earth filled with the flow of water.

Before she left, Murtankala covered the islands she had created with plants and filled the land and sea with living creatures. Finally the land was prepared for her children and for the generations of Tiwi who followed.

Anyone who goes bush on Bathurst or Melville Island, especially in the dry season, will see for themselves that even to this day the Tiwi are grateful to old Murtankala. They love their bush tucker.

Of course there are seasonal foods, but certain fruits and animals are procurable the year round. The islands have long stretches of clean, white beaches. In the north there is rainforest with falls and pools of crystal-clear water. There is a swath of useless country, poor and waterless, but there still remain wide tracts of hunting land. Today the Tiwi hunt with shotguns instead of spears and throwing stricks.

Men go to sea in small boats the year round for turtle. They spear them and then either jump into the water with knives to finish them off or run the boat to tire the turtles, making it easier to get them aboard. The animals are rendered helpless if tossed over turn turtle, and can be kept fresh for days with the help of a few buckets of water.

The cooking of the turtle on the beach is something of a ritual in itself, and if any of the hunters happen to have the turtle as a totem they will do the turtle dance before the feast.

The custom is for the family group to forage together. While the men fish, the women and children prod the sand on the beaches for turtle eggs, or slush through the swamps hunting mud crabs and the mangrove worm, which is swallowed raw as it is pulled from the tree.

At the beginning of the dry season, Seagull Island, just off the northern coast of Melville, is covered with the spotted eggs of the tern. The Tiwi rate them as good eating.

Goannas are mostly caught after the fires are lit early in the dry season, carpet snakes and flying foxes when they can be caught napping.

Yams are dug in the dry season and bush potatoes in the wet. Numerous fruits are gathered, including various white, green and black berries, billy-goat plums, white love apples and native red apples. There is also the bush pumpkin, which requires a lot of preparation before it is edible. The middle is thrown away, as it is very peppery, then the pumpkin is cooked in a ground oven overnight. The skin is dried and boiled and then the water is drunk to make one's chest and heart strong.

Geese, possums and bandicoots are also hunted, mainly at night.

As soon as Kumunupinari, the dry season, gets under way the thoughts of the Tiwi turn to wallaby hunts. (There are no large species of kangaroo on the islands.) The spear grass is high at the end of the Wet and a wallaby is hard to spot, so men from several households organise a joint hunt. The grass is set on fire over a large area and the animals, dazed by the smoke and confusion, are rounded up and killed.

The wallaby carcasses are strung up on a low branch of a tree and gutted, then the fur is singed off. The specialities, including the heart and the liver, are cooked separately, with the wallaby flattened out on the fire inside facing down.

In the ashes the women sometimes bury zamia palm nuts they have collected. Next morning the outer shells of the nuts are cracked with a piece of ironwood, and the kernels crushed and heaped into a fanned palm leaf. These are then placed in a running stream for three days to get the poison out. After this the nuts are ready for eating with sugarbag.

Bush tucker comes in many forms, but tea bags
and four-wheel drives are a modern innovation.

38

An invitation from the Puautjimi people, who portray the dingo in their family Dreaming dance, to go with them to gather mussels, longbums (a type of shellfish) and, maybe, some delectable muranga yams.

We leave camp in the cool of the very early morning in a small dinghy but by the time we pull the boat onto the beach at the end of the trip the sun is blazing.

We carry a shovel, knives, some plastic buckets and bottles of drinking water. We walk through soft and slightly sandy soil under small trees which give very little shade. Marie and Edwina scrutinise the ground for a spindly, dried-out vine that leads to the prized muranga yam which could be as much as two metres below the surface. Marie spies the telltale vine. It is usually the women who find them. The men do the digging. It is hard work in the equatorial sun. 'I can't understand why you don't go to the island store for your food,' I needle. 'You can't get good bush tucker like this there,' says Stanley. 'There's nothing like it, and it's good for you, too.'

Later we cross a very smelly swamp. I am reluctant, even afraid, to go further but Marie eggs me on, showing me where to step. 'The pigs like this place,' she tells me. I am not surprised, but I do not fancy facing a savage boar with big tusks while I am knee-deep in mud. Now I know why the men are carrying guns, even though we are only gathering yams and mussels. There's a splash nearby and a rustle in the reeds. 'That's pigs,' somebody says, but I only get to see them in the distance.

We reach a forest of mangroves. It is gloomy, with only filtered light, and the stench is terrible. It is seemingly without life. You can see the high tide waterline on the tree trunks. We clamber slowly over the roots and I have visions of being stuck here when the tide comes in. With sticks we poke around in the mud for mussels. How could gourmet food live here? Soon the buckets are full.

Edwina and Alfonso have gone ahead and by the time we catch up they have caught a copper snake and have started a fire to cook it on. It is the first time I have eaten snake, a flaky, fishy sort of meat.

Alfonso Puautjimi digging for muranga yam.
Sometimes they are buried two metres below the surface.

It's hard work looking for the muranga yam but
the taste of this much-prized delicacy is worth the
effort.

The Tiwi share their islands with a growing population of salt-water crocodiles. They abound among the mangroves at river entrances but they also find their way up the rivers, lurk in freshwater billabongs and cruise the open sea. They are a peril the Tiwi have learned to live with, especially since 1972 when the Australian government imposed a ban on crocodile shooting.

The 'saltie' is renowned as a silent and efficient killer. Brother Pye puts it this way: Both ends of the croc are dangerous. If you trust either end you can end up in the middle.

Tiwi storytellers have many tales about the yirrikipayi, their word for the most feared reptile of all. Here are two of them:

Gemma Tipuamantumeri was rescued from the jaws of a crocodile when her husband jammed his thumbs into the eyes of the killer. This was in the topless era and old-timers recall the telltale scars on her body.

Louis Munkara had no choice but to fight a croc with his axe in the muddy mangrove swamp near Fourcroy on Bathurst Island. He brought home the skin to back up his story.

In the past there were numerous stories of Tiwi taking on crocodiles single-handed and without a gun. Apparently, it was not unlike a boxing contest with a great deal of sidestepping. The croc did not always lose, but he mostly did.

They also tell the story of the famous Tiwi artist, Declan, who was working as a spotter and canoe-paddler back in 1956 for a professional crocodile hunter, Fred Bennett. They already had three dead crocodiles in the dugout canoe when Fred shot

A 'saltie'. It pays to keep more than one step ahead
of these unpredictable and often deadly reptiles.

an eighteen-footer through the head. They had to tow it behind. When they reached the shore Declan was in the water holding the (apparently dead) monster's paw, when the croc grabbed his forearm. Declan screamed and Fred pumped more bullets into the croc but it refused to let go. So Fred jumped into the water and kicked the creature in the belly. The croc let go at once. As the story goes, it was indignant at being hit below the belt.

Some Tiwi will tell you (and only half in jest) that after crocodiles the thing they fear most in the bush is the pamannuans, the little people. Pamannuans have big heads and ears and wide mouths. Like snakes, they come out at night. You can find Tiwi today who will swear that they have seen them sitting on stumps or logs, pointing and laughing and scaring the wits out of anyone who chances along.

Brother Pye says the Tiwi should be referred to as the Irish Aborigines because of the common belief in fairies and because of other common traits, such as their love of song and fun-making, their outgoing nature, and the fact that they also enjoy an occasional donnybrook.

He tells of the story of Christopher Tipungwuti (who later became an elder), who claimed he saw one of the little people while he was climbing a bloodwood tree six miles from Nguiu. He had been getting bush honey, he said, when the strange little man poked his head out of a hole in the tree. Christopher ran all the way back to Nguiu: and that was in 1945, before the Tiwi were given the right to drink.

The tree is still known as the pamannuas tree.

The deep pool at the bottom of the Taracumbe Falls, on the west side of Melville, is one of the places on the islands where you can swim without fear of crocodiles, sharks and the deadly box jellyfish.

We are on our way there. The back of the truck is full of young boys and men. We try to get there before the black sky opens up but halfway there the rains come. The boys shield themselves with green garbage sacks. 'It stops the rain from hurting us,' they say. We keep driving. The track has turned into a torrent.

By the time we get there the rain has stopped but it has swollen the falls. They thunder over the rocks, a white backdrop to the black figures of the boys leaping from the cliffs into the pool. Lush ferns, deliciously cool water, no crocodiles. Heaven.

ANOTHER TIME, ANOTHER PLACE

Our headlights panic a buffalo, which crashes off through the bush. Scared wallabies cross our track ahead. The trees fly past and the tall spear grass flicks against the sides of the truck.

Some foresters from Pickataramoor are taking me to Goose Creek on Melville.

We beat dawn to the dinghy waiting to take us along the creek that now, in the Wet, is a swirling river. It gets its name from the magpie geese that live in their thousands along its banks. With four in the boat plus my camera case we are sitting close to the water but no-one seems to worry. We watch the sunrise unfold the scene.

The water is a perfect mirror, reflecting the old gums, the pandanus and mangrove trees. We glide through a sward of delicately coloured pale purple, pink and white waterlilies. No motor, the tide tugs us along.

We bump something. 'Don't move,' I am warned. 'We have just hit a crocodile. There she goes.' A dark mass disappears among the lilies. 'This is a nursery for baby crocs. Fish galore. It's mostly barra and salmon and, of course, we're not short on water snakes. Melville is the home of snakes.'

The sky is still pink, the clouds are forming into towers. A sea eagle perched in a tree follows our progress. The river gets wider, the banks lower and the trees fade away as we approach the sea entrance. Magpie geese honk overhead. We watch a lone jabiru, a giant black and white bird with bright red legs, standing motionless in shallow water, waiting for a breakfast of fish to come along.

Eventually we have to turn around. Now we need the motor to go back upstream. The noise shatters the spell of paradise.

A special piece of paradise: no crocodiles.

Esther Babui, who was educated in Ballarat, Victoria, and became the first female Tiwi teacher, has been able to put together something of her grandmother's way of life:

'Of course, there was no marriage ceremony, the girl belonged to her husband when she was born. It was all arranged before her birth.

'When a baby was about to be born the mother-to-be was led away from the camp and her husband by the other women, who put her in the shade and lit a fire.

'The women laid her down gently and rubbed her hard on the back and the front. Paperbark and ironwood leaves were used for the delivery of the baby and cycad palm leaf to cut the cord.

'The newborn baby was laid to sleep in warm ashes while the mother was cared for, and after an hour or more the baby was given to the mother for feeding.

'It was the Tiwi law that the husband must not see his wife from the time of birth until the baby was two moons old. During this time the father was only allowed to wave to the baby from a distance. Women relatives went hunting for crabs, oysters, mangrove worms and yams to keep the mother's breasts supplied with milk.

'When the baby reached three or four moons the mother took it back to the main camp and it was only then that the father was allowed to hold his baby.'

Today, most weddings are still arranged carefully along the right marriage line. Even for those who choose their partner it is not a completely random choice because the traditional skin groupings must be borne in mind.

The couple is married in the church with the father of the bride—dressed in Tiwi naga (ceremonial dress) and painted up with intricate designs on his body and face—bringing the bride down the aisle. Usually, the ceremony is followed by prolonged wailing, especially if either the bride's mother or father are dead. The family Dreaming dances follow, then the feast.

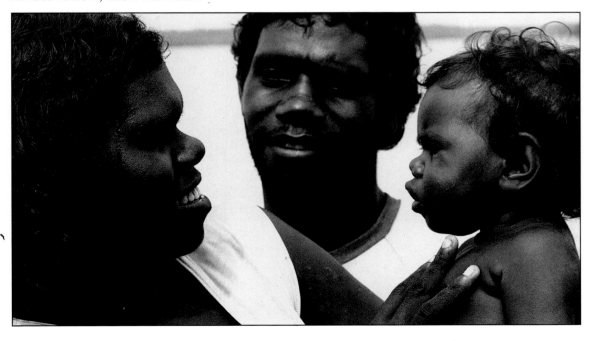

A young modern Tiwi family; modern in that Mary Elizabeth and Jan chose to marry each other.

Naturally, the Tiwi have evolved their own medicine and many of their cures have been handed down from generation to generation. Some were fairly drastic: toothache was cured by either knocking out the tooth or by putting something red-hot on it. A cut to the head to 'let it out' cured a headache, while the treatment for eye trouble was to spit in it. Maggots were used to clean wounds, especially in the ears.

Although Medicare is available to them today, some Tiwi people are just as likely to go walkabout in the bush if they are sick or in pain and put their faith in the old remedies. Jimijinga leaves are boiled for someone with a sore throat, a cough or chest pains. The water is drunk and the leaves are chewed. Better still is a dose of boiled cheeky mangrove worm. The Tiwi swear by it for any virus; it is their wonder drug. To stop diarrhoea they simply scrape the top of a reddish brown ant bed and swallow a little three times daily, or chew some turtiyangini, which is white clay. For backache they just scrape some hot ashes onto a large leaf and apply firmly. And they say sores dry up when bathed with the residue solution from the boiled-up leaves and bark of a particular mangrove tree.

The Tiwi heed various signs of danger. If they suffer sudden pain it tells them that one of their relatives is sick or that something is wrong with them. An accidental knock on the face means that either their brother or sister is in trouble. It is the same message if a dog bites them on the leg. Sudden rain during the dry season is believed to be the rain of the dead and a warning that someone is about to die.

A story is told how in the Dreamtime a Tiwi man drinking from the big lake at Mawuntuwu was swallowed up by Ampiji, the rainbow serpent.

'And so today,' the storyteller winds up, 'people are afraid to swim in that lake. When we go there we first call out to that Ampiji. And when we have eaten sugarbag near there we don't drink water from that lake and we don't wash our hands there. Over at that place we don't kill water goanna and we don't pull waterlily because we don't want to disturb Ampiji. When young women have their period they don't go near that lake. When we see the rainbow in the sky, then that is Ampiji. Women who are pregnant or who have newborn children will not go near water then because they are afraid that if Ampiji is there she may swallow them.'

In the case of old people, Australian-born anthropologist C. W. M. Hart has reported that the 'covering up' custom was still in vogue within the tribe when he was doing his fieldwork among the Tiwi in 1928 and 1929. It was a means of getting rid of ancient females, a practice not uncommon among hunting and gathering peoples.

He describes how a hole was dug in some lonely place and how, with the agreement of the old woman's sons and brothers, she was put into the hole, which was filled until only her head was showing. Everybody went away for a day or two and then went back to the hole to discover, to their great surprise, that the ancient one was dead, having been too feeble to raise her arms from the earth. Nobody had 'killed' her. Her death in Tiwi eyes was a natural one. After all, she had been alive when the relatives last saw her.

Paru is a settlement away from the hustle and bustle, away from the noise of children playing. It is self-imposed exile for some of the older people—mainly women.

To get there we have to cross the Apsley Strait from Bathurst to the southern end of Melville. Some boys take us over in their dinghy. We land on muddy mangrove banks. The heat is heavy under the grey sky. There is no movement in the air. Waves lick at the mangrove roots, crabs click noisily as they make a hasty retreat. As we climb to higher land my camera gear puts on weight. From the deep shade of some mango trees we see huts. Camp dogs announce our arrival before we can call out. Gerardine explains to me: You never just arrive at somebody's place. You must call out as you approach. Otherwise you could frighten people and, perhaps, get a hostile reception.

Nearly everybody is asleep under the trees. What else is there to do under the midday sun? After their initial sniff or two the dogs have also flopped down again. We say hello and have a chat.

Marjorie—a Tiwi woman with hair that has gone yellow—wanders over to the water tank. She pours a mugful over her hair, and it runs down over her shoulders and her breasts, to be soaked up in the skirt. She does it again but there is no escape from the heat, not even in the shade of the trees.

Another woman stirs the ashes in the fireplace and pulls out a cooked fish. She peels back the skin and eats the flesh off the bones. The rest goes to the dogs.

My friends say they have come to visit one of the old ladies they know but there is a shaking of heads. 'She is not well and does not want to see anybody. We have tried to talk to her. Anyway, her dogs won't let you get near her.'

Views such as this are commonplace on Melville
Island

Later we are shown some fine carvings done by these secluded women. 'Why do they choose to live here on their own?' I ask Gerardine. 'They like the peace and quiet away from too much noise and the children, and they have each other for company. Sometimes they visit the village. Also, relatives bring over food.'

Before long we are back on the beach calling for a boat to take us back to the nerve centre, Nguiu.

Marjorie Wonamirri at Paru.

A wife's unfaithfulness, the story goes, began the link between religion and art. It was way back just after creation, even before there was death, and so there was no call for the carved and decorated burial posts that represent Tiwi art today in Australian galleries and in books.

The legend is a melancholy one. The wayward wife was Pima and Purrukuparli her wronged husband. He was the eldest son of Murtankala, the creator woman.

It appears that Purrukuparli's brother, Japarra, the moon man, was without a wife. When Pima went out with her baby, Jinani, to hunt for bush tucker, Japarra followed and tempted her to spend the day in the bush with him. She left her son in the shade but the sun shifted and the heat and hunger killed him.

When Purrukuparli found out what had happened he was furious. Japarra pleaded that he be given a chance to heal the boy. It would take three days.

'No,' said Purrukuparli. 'We have got to follow my son. Nobody returns now, we will all die. You will all follow my son.'

Then Purrukuparli and Japarra fought with forked clubs and Japarra was stabbed in the eye. Japarra then changed himself into the moon, to be eternally reincarnated after three days of darkness every month. Today you see the marks that Purrukuparli inflicted with his club as dark spots on the moon.

Unhappy Pima was left in the bush. She turned into a stone curlew, the wailing bird, and wanders the night calling in remorse for her dead son.

The Pukumani mourning ceremony was held following the death of Purrukuparli. It was conceived, according to legend, by Tokwampini, an ancestral man/bird. This established the ritual for all future Tiwi mourning ceremonies. Ever since, the Tiwi have carved grave posts for people who die, painted themselves and danced sorrowfully as a farewell. Even after a Roman Catholic funeral service a Pukumani takes place for most Tiwi when they die. This, they say, doubly ensures the safe departure of the soul of the dead person.

The complex Pukumani custom is without doubt the cornerstone of the Tiwi's traditional belief. Anthropologists have stressed that, unlike tribes on the Australian mainland, the Tiwi culture lacked magic or sorcery. Perhaps they never felt the need to conjure up magic to bring rain, point the bone or sing a man to death because, generally, they had a friendly environment of plenty with no neighbouring tribes to threaten them.

They did, however, have taboos to which they adhered religiously. Anything forbidden or untouchable was called Pukumani and these taboos invariably referred to the dead. Bodies of the dead were Pukumani, grave posts were Pukumani, the names of the dead were Pukumani, as well as all the names bestowed by the deceased. When a man named Monday died a few years ago the first day of the week was called 'washing day' until the Pukumani period was over. And after someone called Xavier died, the church choir refused to sing 'Heart of our Saviour'. Sister Tess recalls that when a man named Umbrella died she had to refer to her brolly as a rainstick.

In the past close relatives of dead people had to abstain from sex, could not touch food at all and had to be fed by non-mourners.

The Tiwi adhered to the strict conditions of Pukumani apparently without dissent. Apart from these taboos related to the dead the Tiwi were not concerned with religion in their everyday life. It would appear that Pukumani observance was more a matter of respectability than it was a case of pleasing the spirits.

So, it was around death that the Tiwi wove their most elaborate web of ritual.

Babies were not really given funeral ceremonies at all and children had small ones, but young adult males and all women rated funerals of medium size. Old men had the biggest funerals of all.

All bodies were wrapped in bark and buried within twenty-four hours of a person dying. The big occasion was the mourning Pukumani which took place some time later, usually in the dry season when people could travel.

Before the final Pukumani there was the smoking ceremony to chase away the spirit of the dead person.

Weathered old Pukumani poles keep watch over
this sacred burial site next to the sea at Karslake
on Melville Island.

My friend Gerardine points to a house as we walk through the village. She is solemn. 'Someone is dying there. I think he will go tonight.' Tiwi rarely use people's names, and never if that person could be Pukumani tomorrow. I cannot contain my curiosity. 'How do you know?' Gerardine shakes her head. 'It will be tonight.' This man is very old and has been ill for a long time, confined to a wheelchair. Also, he has a pacemaker! Gerardine says so.

The man does die during the night. All his family, mobs of people as the Tiwi say, spend the last evening with him. Tiwi are never left alone in their hour of death. All his relatives from both islands have gathered. They camp around the house under the trees, singing, telling stories and playing cards. Then, at death, the wailing starts. It can be heard for miles. Relatives of the same skin group are preparing for the funeral. White clay is mixed into a soft paste. A branch with leaves is dipped into the paste and then the mourner is lashed with the branch until the body is covered with the shapes of leaves. This body painting must be carried out by someone of a different skin group.

The deceased is lying under the trees surrounded by his relatives and friends. The wailing seems to intensify the shimmering heat. All around me the Tiwi are rocking to and fro, crying. Some faint and others go to their aid, then they carry on mourning. The children are bewildered and cry too. The camp dogs throw back their heads and howl.

Unnerved, I just watch. Even with permission there is no way I could pick up my camera, focus and click away.

Some time later the body is put into a coffin and carried to the cemetery. The dead man is given a Christian burial.

Next day there is a smoking ceremony at the man's house. Victoriana, the widow, is seated with relatives on the grass outside. I remind her that I photographed her husband last August in the bush. I knew him well. May I photograph the ceremony? She recognises me and nods.

The Tiwi elders arrive dressed in traditional naga. They make a small fire outside and burn green branches which give off clouds of heavy smoke. First the small children are waved through the smoke to cleanse and protect them against evil spirits. Then the burning leaves are carried in an old oil drum through the house, filling it with smoke. The ceremonial dancers are the first to enter the house, stomping in a rhythm to the chants. The relatives follow, wailing and crying. Later in the day Father Leahry arrives and waves incense through the house, a second smoking ceremony. This one is Christian. The Tiwi accept this as added protection against evil spirits.

From the time of his death the name and all talk about the deceased is Pukumani for at least a year.

Some six months from now there will be a Pukumani ceremony with ceremonial dancing. The Pukumani poles are erected next to the grave. Not all the dead are buried in cemeteries. If somebody dies from a snakebite, for instance, the grave and the protective Pukumani posts will be in the bush near the place of death.

The smoking ceremony, with its wailing, singing
and dancing, can be quite an unnerving experience
for the outsider.

After the smoking ceremony the personal grave posts are carved and painted and later there is a week of relationship dancing, calling all the people to the placing of the posts around the grave site. This marks the end of the mourning period. The bark baskets that carried the food and the presents for the Pukumani workers are then placed on top of the posts.

The earliest recorded posts would not have attracted much outside attention. They were merely tree trunks to the uninitiated. In any case the carvings created with mussel shell scrapers and stone axes would not have been very elaborate after a few years, especially if they were tough ironwood posts. Even Auguste Rodin would not have made much of an impression on ironwood or woollybutt trees with these implements.

Then came the Tiwi's iron age. They got their hands on a few axes and some scraps of iron from shipwrecked vessels during the nineteenth century and the carving on their grave posts became more elaborate. The posts developed ears and breasts and a thin waisted section. They were decorated with a complex arrangement of dots, cross-hatching, circles and lines. Obviously, they were representations of people.

Over the last thirty years some fine carvers and painters have emerged among the Tiwi. A feature of their work is their innovative approach. The only explanation they have for their original designs and carving styles is that they get their inspiration from their ancestor, Purrukuparli.

Marie Evelyn and husband Stanley Puautjimi
working together on Tiwi art.

Tiwi traditional painting consists of bold lines, circles and dots in a geometric design. The only colours used are black, obtained from charcoal, and white, yellow and red ochres from Bathurst Island cliffs. Their patterns often depict sites of stories of mythological significance involving ancestors who were changed into animals or birds.

Barbed ceremonial spears, traditionally made for burial ceremonies, copy the double rows of barbs that grew along the tail of the ancestral crocodile. Early collectors reported that these delicately carved spears were fashioned with a shell scraper and took as long as three months to complete.

These days they have borrowed from the mainland the idea of painting portable sheets of bark. In their days of isolation they used to occupy themselves during the long wet season by painting on the inside of their bark shelters, lying on their backs like Michelangelo.

One school of Tiwi artists is now turning out stylised birds, especially the jabiru. This bird, according to Tiwi mythology, was around at the same time as Purrukuparli. One day a jabiru was speared by a hunter but flew off. In distress, she urinated into the sea, turning the fresh water salty. After this the Tiwi had to go inland for their water.

Robert Malangwa's carving of a stingray.

The busiest place in downtown Nguiu on Bathurst is the workshop set up to encourage traditional art among the Tiwi.

Their reggae music finds me as I approach. Coming out of the glare, my eyes have to adjust. Ceiling fans hum but it is still stiflingly hot. The air smells of paint. Artists crouch over their screens. There is not much talking. Most of the screen printers and designers are young men. There are both black and white instructors.

At lunchtime they sit outside under the trees playing draughts and listening to music.

Creation of various art works is an integral part of Tiwi life today. The bark baskets, wood carvings and funeral poles all carry symbolic geometric designs painted in bright ochre colours. They are abstract and each artist has their own interpretation, just as they each want to relate their own statement on Tiwi life.

The workshop, called Tiwi Design, is housed in two large sheds close to the Apsley Strait. Artists collect their own materials: ironwood, barks, pandanus, ochres, seeds and feathers. There is a display area where finished works are sold.

The pottery workshop is in another shed. Carving and painting is usually done outdoors. A great many artefacts are made in and around their homes all over the islands by women.

The final results are praised and criticised, sometimes rejected. There is a 'Keeping Place', a kind of museum and gallery, in Nguiu for special works of art.

Tiwi women artists with their tungas posing in front
of the 'Keeping Place'.

The most talented and most prolific of the Tiwi carvers was Declan Arakike Apuatimi, who came from Melville Island where ironwood was his matrilineal clan totem. As a boy he had an urge to work with this wood and started carving spears and fluted clubs. He left his homeland to join the pearling fleet as a young man and it was not until he was well into middle age that he became a serious carver.

Declan's father had carved grave posts and ceremonial spears for Pukumanis but Declan created his masterpieces for the outside world market. Solid figures with face and body segmented into lively panels of dots, cross-hatching and staring almond eyes typified his style of carving. It was Declan who first carved figures with tiered faces. Most of them had three faces on top of each other. His best work was done in the late 1970s.

The quiet little man, who was also a renowned dancer and singer, was quite ingenuous about the inspiration for his figure carvings. 'Just what comes into my mind,' he used to say. There was one carving of a female figure complete with a thatch of pubic hair, which Declan revealed after it had been sold in a Sydney gallery as an 'Aboriginal love goddess' to be his conception of a white woman in Darwin who bought a lot of his work.

After Declan died in 1985 there was a memorial exhibition of his art.

The art of Declan Apuatimi. Left: Purrukuparli and Pima. Right: Pima.

56

I see him first walking along the beach with his head down kicking stones into the sea. Now and then he picks one up and skips it across the water. Slowly, his slight figure slips from sight.

Next day he is standing under a mango tree throwing stones at the fruit to bring them down. Then he sits in the shade, alone, dreaming. A girl comes by and sits with him. They talk a little. Then they both seem to be dreaming. No giggling, no fighting, no crying.

Now Tony is my friend and I know him to be different from the other children. He is often alone. When he sees me he comes over loaded with questions. He points to my camera. 'What's that? What does it do? Where is Canberra? Where is Germany? Can I go there? Can we drive to Germany tomorrow? Why is your hair so yellow? You are not so old. Why do you brush your teeth? Can I do that too?'

The next day I buy Tony a toothbrush. Maybe his friends will tease him about that. He may be a loner at times but he is also popular and has a following among his peers.

Tony Apuatimi is eleven, and is the last offspring of Declan, Tiwi artist of distinction who died four years ago. Declan's carvings are exhibited in museums and galleries all over the world. He was a man of importance so only now has the period of Pukumani come to an end. For those four years Tony could not speak of his father; nobody could.

After I return to Canberra I receive a letter from Tony telling me how he went to Darwin to see his father's paintings and carvings in the museum. The boy has many brothers and sisters who all have children. He moves from one household to another.

I learn from a friend that since I left Tony sits in a tree and has telephone conversations with me . . . 'Ring, ring . . . Hello Heide, how are you? . . . Good one . . . When are you coming back?' He calls often. I receive a letter saying: 'When I grow up I will be a pilotman, then I can fly to Canberra.'

I keep all of his little drawings. He has a good eye and a fresh perspective on the world. One day he will be famous like his father.

Tony Apuatimi has inherited his father's artistic talent.

Second only in importance to the Pukumani is the Kurlama ceremony, centred around a variety of yam of that name covered with wispy roots. Like the ritual of the grave posts this custom is pure Tiwi. Nothing like either of these ceremonies existed in the culture of the Australian mainland Aborigines.

Kurlamas are staged around February, towards the end of the Wet. Just when the yams ripen is the key factor. The ceremony goes on for three days and three nights and there is much singing, dancing and feasting.

The general idea behind the occasion is to help heal hurts of the past year and to express sorrow at various events that may have occurred—something of a confessional. It keeps the clan together. Also, ancestors are remembered. Some of the ritual is to ensure good health and plentiful bush food in the coming year. The little spirit people, the nyingawi, are the mythical force behind the ceremony. Much care is taken to stick to the ritual.

On the first day men and women performing the Kurlama gather around the sacred ground marked out, the kurluwukari, all with painted bodies. Children are taboo at this stage. New songs are composed. The leader always begins the singing with the other men joining in and tapping sticks. The women sing the same song on a higher note but with the same beat as the men. At each interval grief and sorrow is expressed.

Then the men go into the bush to gather the kurlamas. The Tiwi call them 'cheeky' because, unlike the ordinary yam, they are toxic and need to be cooked with care before they are edible. They are not staple diet. The yams, hairy with roots, are very carefully dug out for the ceremony. The roots must be intact; if there is damage there will be sickness.

After the cooking there is the ritual rubbing of the yam on the joints of the body to give strength.

On the third day the yam is eaten. Singing goes on, with the voices of the women like a high-pitched echo. At different stages of the ceremony there is ritual washing

Dancers William Portamini and Stanley Puautjimi
preparing for Kurlama. Black comes from charcoal;
white, yellow and red from riversides and cliffs.

off of paint and then more daubing. Then the children of the head man of the Kurlama do their inherited Dreaming dance.

The Kurlama ends with a loud shout from the gathering.

Traditional initiation ceremonies for young men, which usually coincided with the ripening of the kurlama yams, have faded out in recent decades.

A girl reaching womanhood was never treated as much of an occasion in the tribe. There was no dancing and singing, just some play acting and spear waving which confirmed in public that the girl belonged to the man she had been promised to at birth.

For a boy it was an incredibly long drawn-out affair. It went on for up to twelve years. Much of this time he spent in isolation in the bush with his handful of tutors who taught him the ritual matters a grown man should know. For the little time he spent back home in his village he was involved in periodic ceremonies, when he was ritually advanced from one stage of initiation to the next.

The crucial stage in the cycle was when his pubic hairs were forcibly pulled out. There was never any circumcision as in the initiation of young Aborigines on the Australian mainland. The Tiwi youth was forbidden to talk to females during his initiation years. The fact that all the young men were kept in seclusion and out of the food production unit for so long has amazed anthropologists. One can only wonder whether this system was devised in the interests of the old men intent on keeping the youths away from their many wives.

Tiwi young bloods today have football, Australian Rules style, to take their minds off girls. The Tiwi league teams are called Tuyu (buffaloes), Tarakumbi (magpies), Yirrimuruwu (eagles), Imalu (tigers), Tapalinga (superstars) and Pumaralli (lightning bombers). Many of the stars are sought after by Darwin teams and are flown to the mainland, which their ancestors thought of as the land of the dead, for weekend clashes.

In the remote past there was never a real need for the Tiwi people to band together as a tribe. The two islands were the world and it never even occurred to them that there could be a threat of invasion from other humans or a foreign influence on their way of life. The were *the* people.

If the language they spoke had been a written one the word Tiwi would not have had a capital as does Australian or Eskimo in our language. Tiwi simply means 'us'. Even today they rarely use the word Tiwi to explain who they are. Instead, they say they are a 'Murnupula woman' if they belong to the Murnuppi group, or a 'Jikilawila man' meaning they come from Jikilarruwu. Tiwi closely identify themselves with these groups. There is often confusion because folk tend to get married and move away from their band territories.

The situation has been changing in recent years. The Tiwi have reason to band more closely together as a tribal unit. It is the pressure of progress. Not so long ago they were nomads using bark shelters and rocks for protection from the sun and the rain. It was only in 1929 that the first Catholic marriages took place and the first Tiwi homes were built. They were tiny huts dotting the beach at Nguiu. A Mission project started building more substantial homes after 1952 out of ironwood and cypress pine from the bush, but it was not until 1973 that the first concrete block houses were built for the Tiwi.

The Tapalinga from Bathurst Island play the Imalu from Melville in the grand final. Half-time is an especially welcome respite in the intense tropical heat.

I fly to Milikapiti on Melville to photograph some of the artists there. A fierce sun is mopping up after a cloudburst. Steam sits over the town like a halo. My first call is to the local Council office, but the men are out on a buffalo hunt.

Milikapiti has a population of around 500. There is a school, the Council office, a shop, an adult education centre, a church and a club. Club means pub or hotel and it also means trouble. The Tiwi, like so many indigenous peoples around the globe, have serious problems with alcohol.

Pius Tipungwuti, Chairman of the Milikapiti Council on Melville, is one of the elders trying to combat the 'disease'. His treatment is to keep people out of trouble by making them work. The Tiwi only get their 'sit-down money' (social welfare payments) if they work on community projects—road works, drainage and maintenance of public buildings.

A young couple, Peter and Rosie Simon, offer to put me up for the night. Peter is white. He came to the island as a teacher and fell in love with Rosie, a Tiwi. He is now the Deputy Town Clerk. I get the feeling that life has not been too easy for these two. The Tiwi frown on their people marrying outsiders. The union of two different cultures brings many problems, but Rosie, Peter and their young son are coping.

Early next morning I climb down to the edge of the sea. The villagers have told me to look out for their resident crocodile called George. I spot him cruising way out with eyes and nostrils just above the water. At least I think it is George; they all look the same to me.

The sea is calm and gently laps at the roots of the pandanus and mangroves. I find a shell or two. The rising sun pierces the foliage, rays dancing on the shiny leaves.

Paddy Freddy Puruntatameri is working on a carving in the shade of a huge mahogany when I arrive. He is getting on, about sixty, but is fit without an ounce of fat. His wrinkled, bearded face lights up with a grin. 'Good morning, Mantanga.' Then, in a second, he is back to his furious gouging of a chunky piece of ironwood.

After taking my photographs I move on to find Polly Miller Mungatopi outside her house, breakfasting on mussels cooked in the ashes of a fire. The dogs stay close waiting for leftovers. The old lady sits serenely, reaching down now and again for another morsel until only the empty shells remain.

Further up the track Paddy Henry and his wife Nancy are basking in the early morning sun. It is the only time of the day anybody sits in the open here. Nancy shows me a large, freshly caught mud crab. 'It's for him.' She gives Paddy Henry a beautiful smile. Nancy is much younger than her husband. She was promised to him at the time of her birth when he was already a grown man.

Paddy Henry lost an eye a few years ago working on a carving. His big shoulders tell of the strength he had as a younger man. Nancy is fit, agile and a good hunter and provider. He could not get better care.

It is Pius who takes me, together with some young boys, to Karslake, a burial ground near the sea. Weathered Pukumani poles stand like guards around the graves, the wind from the sea whistling around them. They look stern and solemn and make me feel small and inferior.

Top: A gourmet's breakfast of mussels. Bottom: Ironwood is an extremely tough material to work with. Paddy Henry Ripijingimpi lost an eye when a chunk of the material he was carving hit him in the face.

Time has been halted on the Tiwi islands by Heide's sensitive images. More than that, they carry the clear message to fellow Australians next door, and to others, that the Tiwi cherish their homelands and their way of life.

The thinking Tiwi know in their hearts they have a tough fight on their hands to save their ancient culture from being swamped by outsiders and, as Heide's friend Gerardine might say, the 'humbug' they bring with them.

Not surprisingly, the serious problem on these thirsty tropical islands is the white man's grog. Liquor is threatening to change the Tiwi lifestyle perhaps more than Christianity. On Bathurst, the Nguiu Town Council is trying to combat the problem by restricting drinking hours at the Club (or pub) from 4 p.m. to 9 p.m. and all liquor must be consumed on the premises. The Club is closed on Sundays. No beer is taken into the bush. On Melville, however, drinkers are allowed to take away six cans of beer each.

Excess drinking by some of the men reached the point not so long ago that a

Working for 'sit-down money', Pularumpi, Melville
Island.

group of Tiwi women carried out their threat that they were going off to Darwin and would not return until their husbands stopped drinking. They did not have to stay away for long.

The Tiwi people's impressive representative in the Northern Territory Legislative Assembly is Stanley Tipiloura, the member for Arafura, who sees the situation this way:

'My people believe that our ancestors were responsible for the creation of our country and it was they who handed down to us our rules for living . . . We have ceremonies to look after the well-being and products of our land. Those things penetrate our culture. They often sit uneasily with our acceptance of western culture . . . These modern problems, which to some extent come from the mainland, are the more difficult because we already have our own culture . . . Through our education system and the work of the Tiwi Land Council we now tackle these troubles with the same confidence as do the mainlanders.'

Stanley Tipiloura, MLA.

Aloysius Puantulura.

None of the Tiwi elders is more highly respected than Aloysius Puantulura. I want to say goodbye to him and his wife, Mena. Their bush camp is a three-hour drive from Nguiu 'as long as you don't get bogged'.

I am alone in the four-wheel drive loaned to me by the fatherly Land Council and it is not long before I am finding it hard to distinguish between the track and the bush, especially while dodging holes dug by wild pigs and making detours around fallen trees.

I come to a patch where they have been burning off. The ground is still hot and smoking. Soon it will be sprouting new grass which will lure the wallabies, number one tucker, but now it is hell. A branch crashes down nearby in a shower of sparks. It is hard for me to see well enough through the veil of smoke to avoid the smouldering stumps.

Out of that hot spot and now I am in the sandy stretch they warned me about. I hit the accelerator and swing madly around the trees and rocks slalom fashion, determined not to get stuck. I sing for comfort: 'If my friends could see me now . . .' If only my mother could see me now.

I'm through. I shout for joy, 'I've done it.' So that was the soft horror stretch. At that moment I hit the mud—sticky, black, stinky mud. The tyres spin and the truck begins to sink. I can hear my mother saying 'Hochmut kommt vor dem Fall.' (Overconfidence comes before the fall.) The ooze of the swamp devours my feet. At least I have the sense to leave my thongs high and dry. Snakes keep crossing my mind as I haul branches, rotten logs and palm leaves under the wheels.

Now I feel I'm being watched. I swing my head, searching, and see a dingo, standing still as time, staring at me through the scrub. I switch on the engine, rock the truck to and fro and, finally, lurch out. I'm smiling by the time I reach camp.

They applaud. 'You've made it . . . and you didn't get bogged.' Mena eyes my mud-caked arms and legs. 'Maybe, yes.' Her smile is kind. Aloysius waves his arm grandly. 'We have fresh water creek.' I gratefully accept his offer of a wash.

The camp is a smattering of shelters made from bark and branches and a few old tents surrounded by a strip of burned out land. 'That's to keep the snakes away,' somebody explained.

I sit and talk with them about their country and their people. Mena is loving and caring. You can see she worships her husband. She looks into my eyes. 'You'll come back, yes?' I nod.

Even now, with all his seventy-nine years, Aloysius, the Foundation Chairman of the Tiwi Land Trust, is handsome and proud.

The white traditional Tiwi beard surrounds his lined face and his eyes seem to look into the future and the past at the same time.

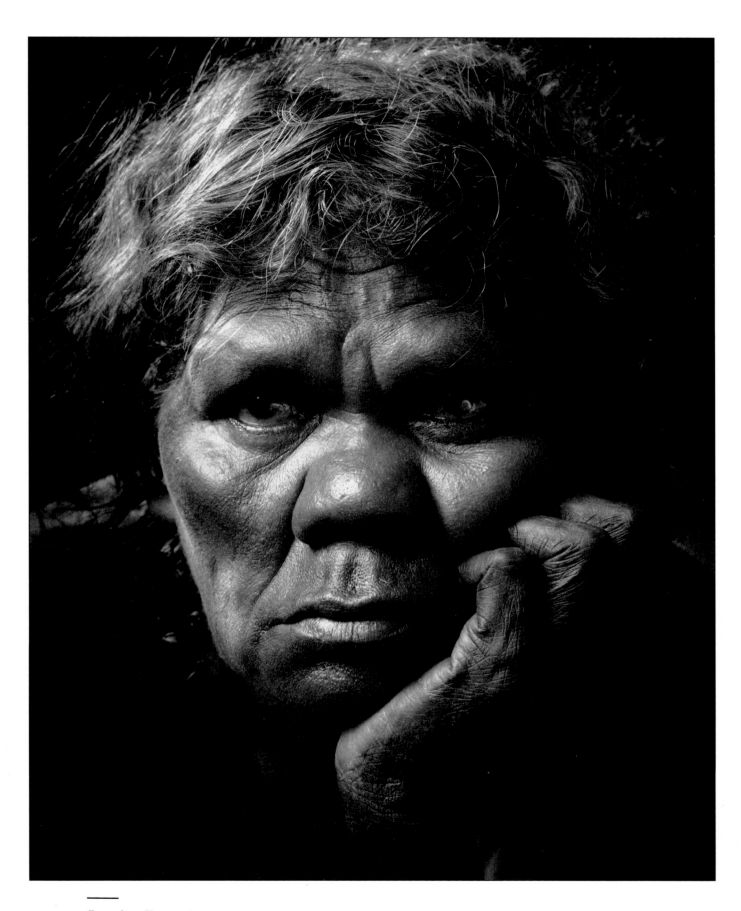

Gerardine Tungatalum.

Bede Tungatalum, Tiwi Design artist.

Justin Puruntatameri, Tiwi elder from Pularumpi.

Barney Tipuamantumirri.

Sarah Puruntatameri, Nguiu.

Betsy Norm Pangarimini shyly covers her toothless
smile.

Marie Carmel Alimankinni and Marie Therese
Palipuaminni of Nguiu. Their strong faces reflect
strong characters.

Seventeen-year-old Sarah Kerinaiua from Nguiu.

Karlene Portamini.

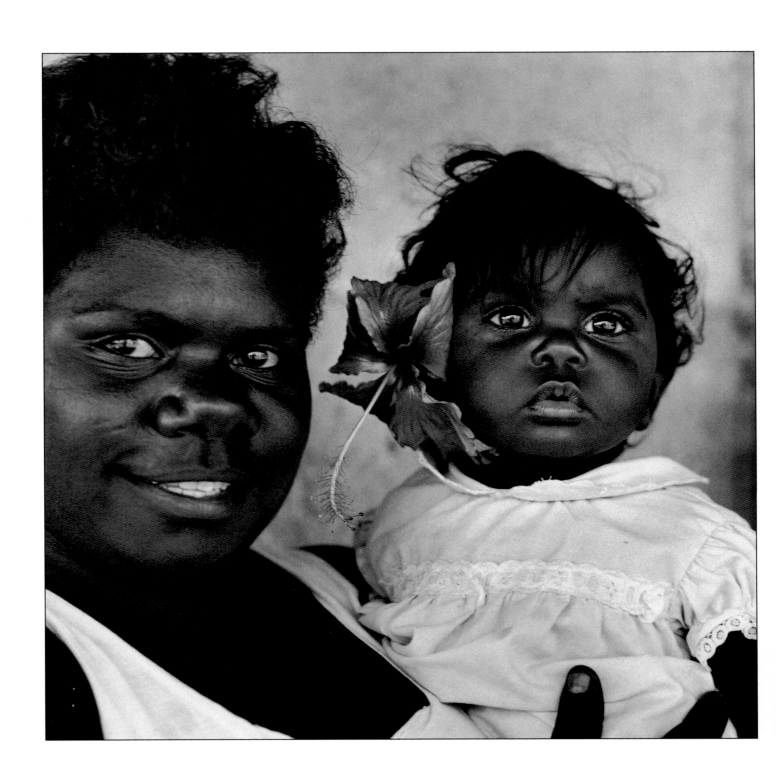

Rachel Kerinaiua with Lorena Tipiloura.

Marie Clare Pilakui holding her tiny baby, Jessie
Bernadine.

Isobel Marego with daughter Samantha at
Milikapiti.

Frances and Mercy Tipakalippa—'in love'.

Timothy Puruntatameri, Pularumpi.

Terence Kantilla.

Phillippa Pupangamirri from Paru. Tiwi figures and
faces often blend in perfectly with the landscape.

Marie Therese Palipuaminni with her crab-claw
pipe, in quiet contemplation.

A Tiwi mother caught in a pensive moment with
her baby.

Constance Mary Tipungwuti and her daughter
Rose.

Tiwi woman, Ada Tipungwuti. There is a special
beauty and dignity in many of the older women.

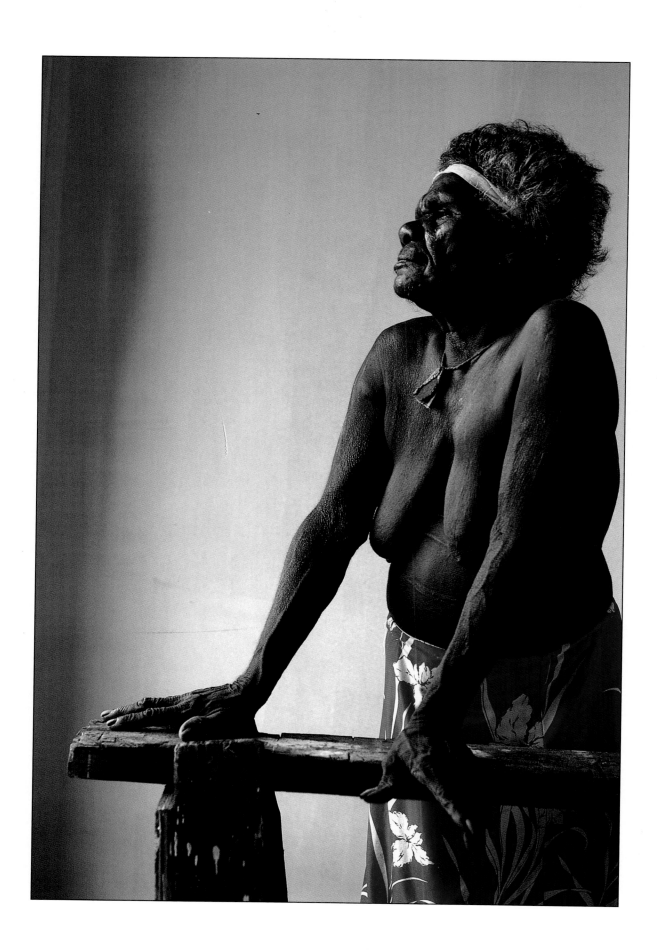

Alfonso Puautjimi in ceremonial decoration. His
head feathers come from the black cockatoo
(Ngaringa).

Paddy Freddy Puruntatameri at a burial place with
the Pukumani poles he carved.

Richard Miller Mungatopi absorbed in his work.

Face and body painting for ceremonies is an
intrinsic part of Tiwi culture.

Body and face painting is art, and Stanley Puautjimi
is one of the finest artists.

Tiwi elders, William Portamini and Stanley
Puautjimi with faces painted for a ritual dance.

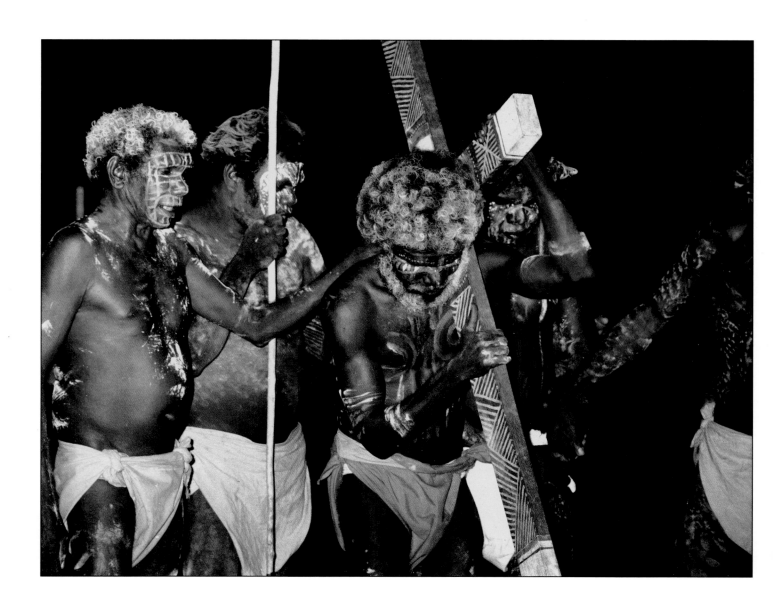

A passion play, performed in honour of the Church.

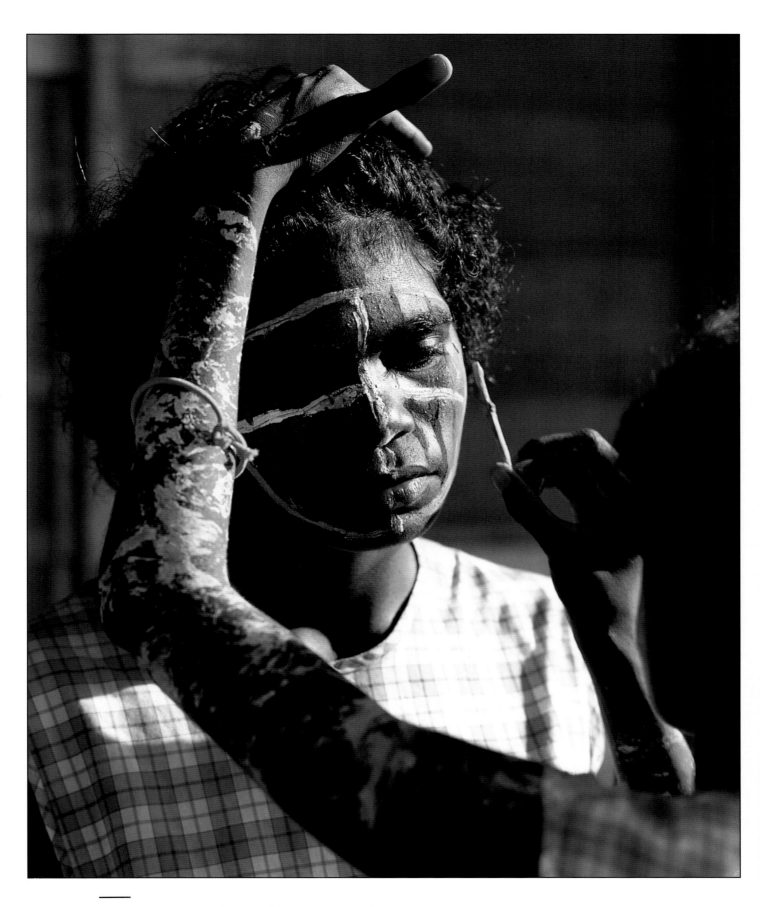

Young girls learning the art of face painting with ochre paints and sticks.

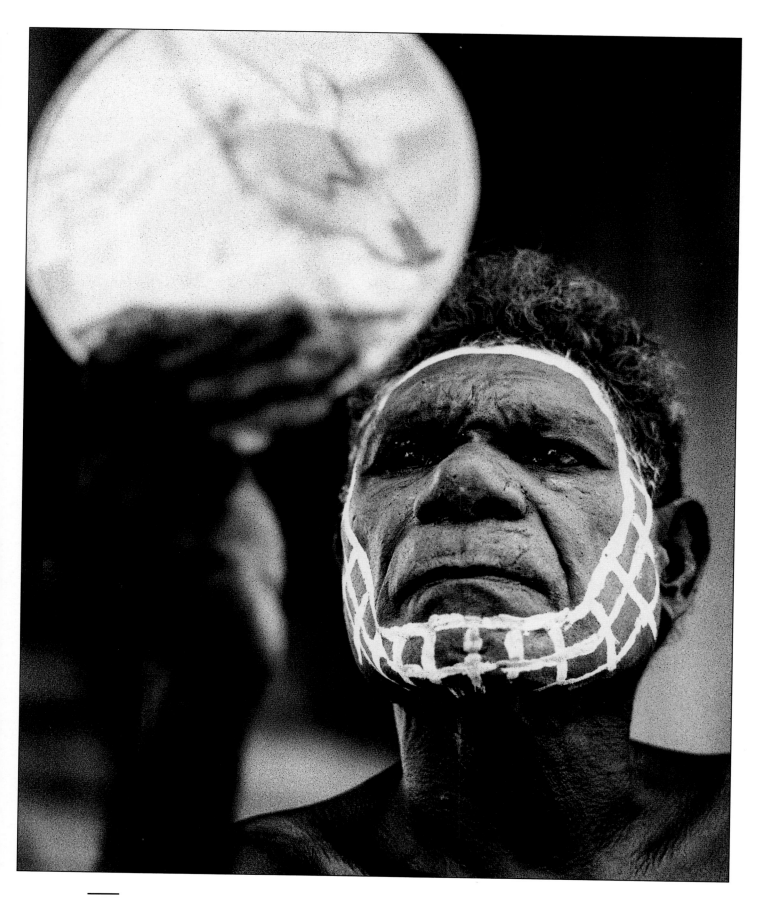

George Norm Pangarimini working with a mirror.

During Kurlama the men sing and the women echo
their voices in a higher pitch.

A 'relationship dance'.

Gerardine Tungatalum is painted by her daughter-in-law, Antonia Kerinaiua, in preparation for a funeral.

Aloysius Puantulura with white ceremonial
cockatoo head feathers called Pimirtiki. The point
that is wound in the hair is made from wallaby
bone. Beeswax is used to glue the feathers to the
bone.

During a Kurlama celebration. James Portamini and
carved snake.

The same man, transformed. Dances, chants and personal decorations are different for each ceremony.

A burial place in the bush on Bathurst Island. Every
now and then weathered Pukumani poles are
decorated with fresh paint.

Every line and every cut on a pole has a meaning.

Sebastian Tipiloura working on a Pukumani pole. Because they are too heavy to be carried a long way, the poles are often carved near the burial site.

Tiwi Design artist, Calistus Babui. The poles are
made from either ironwood or bloodwood.

Leon Puruntatameri from Milikapiti.

Romuald Puruntatameri is a member of the Tiwi
Land Council.

Lorraine Munkara and a tunga she has just completed.

Pius Tipungwuti, President of the Milikapiti
Council and also a carver.

Paddy Freddy Puruntatameri, a carver from the
older generation.

He has cut a perfect piece of bark. He now has
to strip it, then flatten it by placing it under stones
for several days.

Shaun Kerinaiua with a bird figure. Birds feature
in many of the creation tales.

Cyril James Kerinaiua painting his carvings.

Neville Wommatakimmi with carved figures.

John Babui painting a figure he has carved at the
Tiwi Design workshop.

Jock Puautjimi is a gifted carver as well as a potter.

Eddie Puruntatameri from Garden Point, probably
the best potter on the islands. Eddie started the
pottery workshop at Nguiu in 1972.

Alan John Kerinaiua.

Danny Munkara.

Bede Tungatalum with one of his screens. Bede
is one of the founders of Tiwi Design.

Osmond Kantilla, one of the most innovative silk
screen designers.

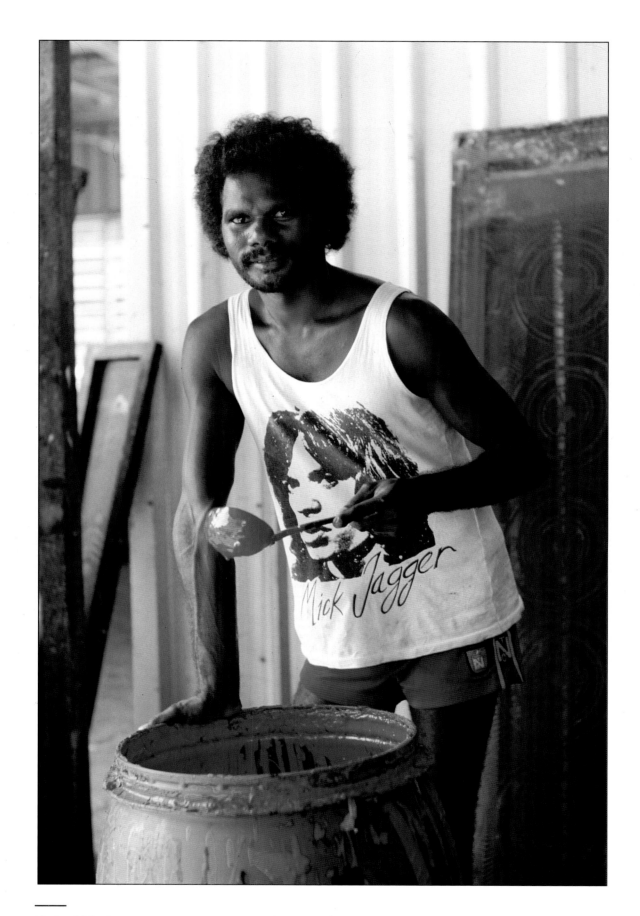

Michael Munkara, a screen printer at Tiwi Design.

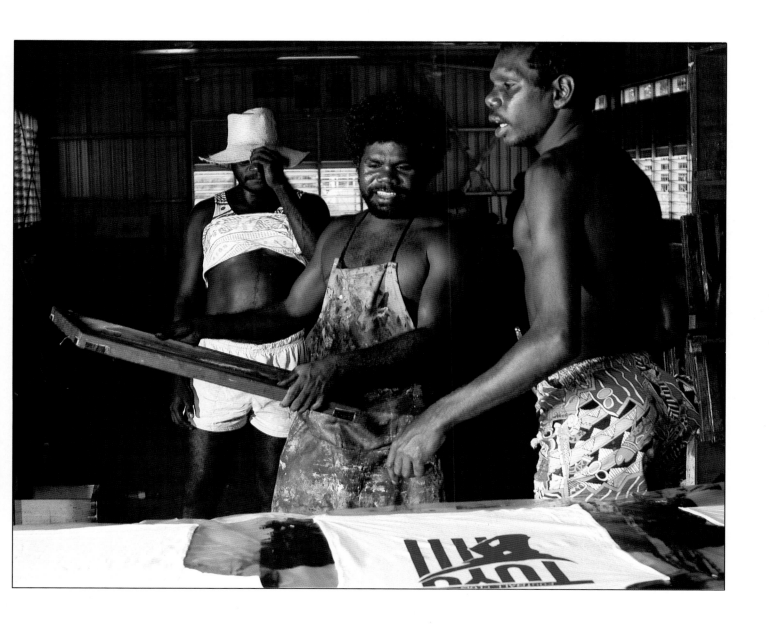

It's hot in the workshop of Tiwi Design and the
ceiling fans don't seem to make much difference.
Dress is strictly casual.

Tiwi Design screen printer Edwin Fernando with
screens.

Screen-printed cotton. Some Tiwi pattern names
are: snake, sun, lizard, worm, yam and stone axe.

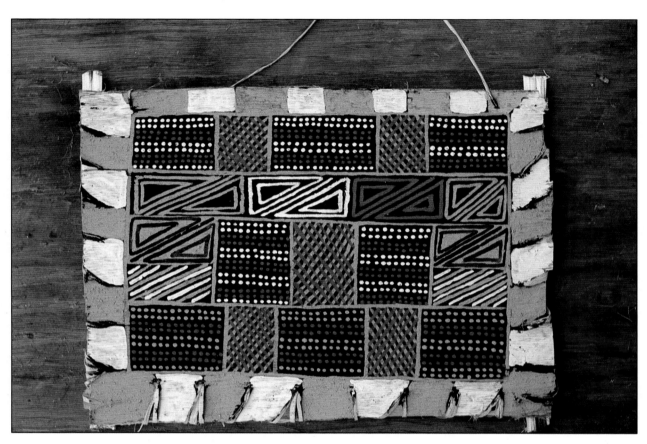

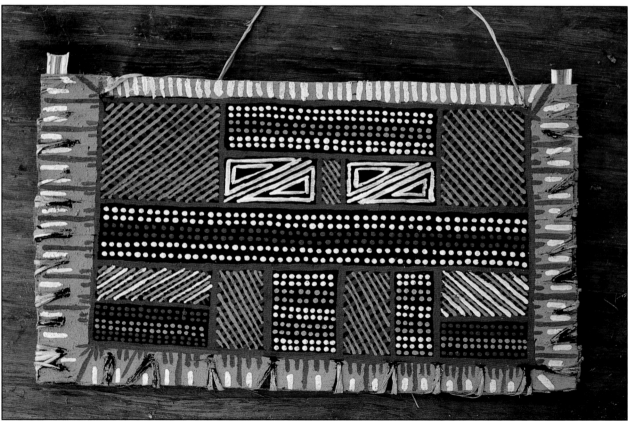

Bark paintings by Gemma Munkara.

Top: 'Yirrajirrima Pamajini' by Irene Babui.
Bottom: Bark painting by Jennifer Tipiloura.

Madeline Puantulura is preparing pandanus leaves
to make armbands and headbands.

Nora Palipuaminni with one of her pandanus
baskets. This work requires much patience as well
as skill.

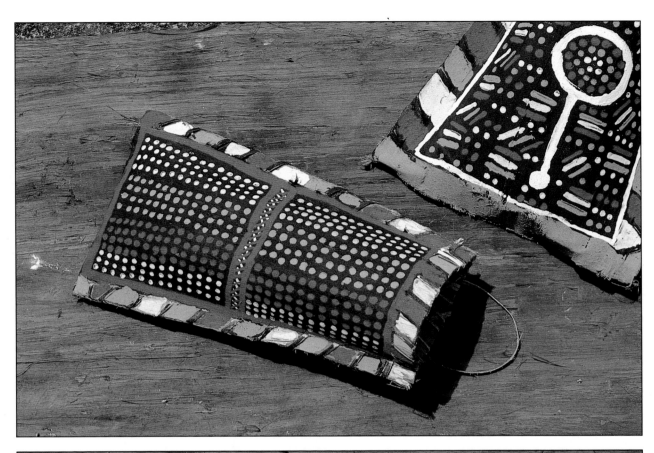

Top: Tungas by Concepta Kantilla. Bottom: Armbands and headbands by Sidonia Munkara, made from the root of the mangrove tree and bound with string made from the pandanus palm.

Top: Turlini (water basket) by Ada Tipungwuti.
Tunga (bark basket) by Dorothy Joy Tipungwuti.
Miyarti (pandanus basket) by Marie Evelyn
Puautjimi. Bottom: Mampini (bark canoe) by
Charlie Puruntatameri.

Purrukuparli by Stanislaus Puruntatameri.

Wayayi (Pima).

A traditional painting of the legendary Rainbow
Serpent.

The simple exterior of the Keeping Place belies
the fantastic collection of artworks it houses. This
is the ceiling collage.

At dusk, colours and shapes take on a different
meaning. This is when parents tell their children
stories of the Dreamtime.

Colombiere Tipungwuti from Pularumpi is a dancer
of the younger generation and he has ambitions
to perform, not just among his people, but for
Australia.

Here he shows the steps of some animal dances,
in front of 'the Big Cloud'.

St Therese's Church on Bathurst Island was built
in 1941 from cypress pines, a native tree of the
island.

Small children and dogs wait outside the church
while Mass is conducted.

Magdalene Kerinaiua, Tiwi writer.

A Tiwi teacher often acts as mother and friend
too.

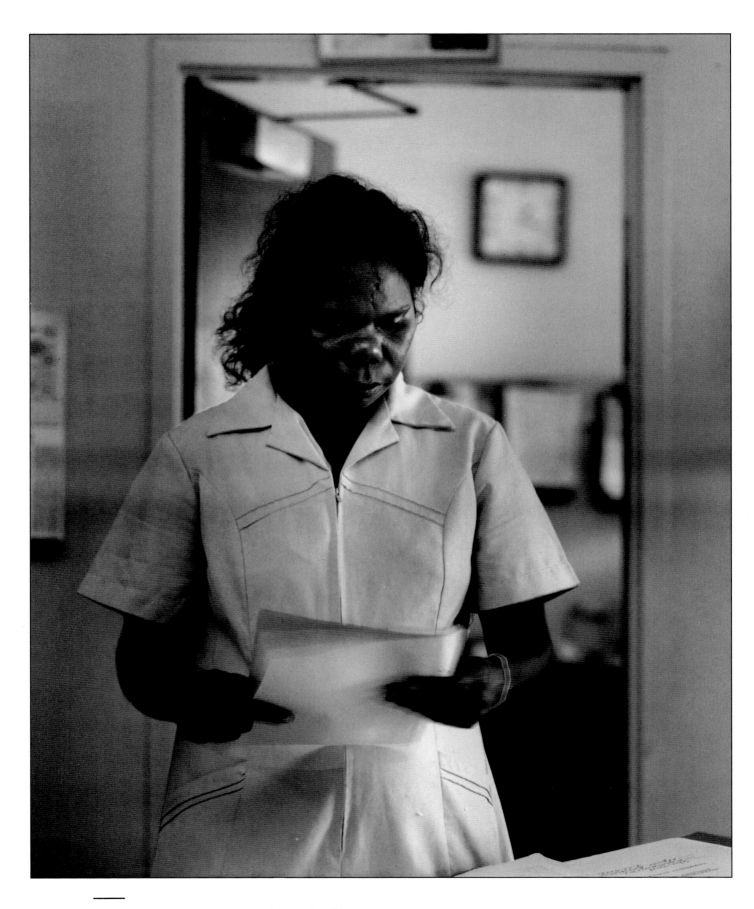

Tiwi nurse Eunice Orsto at the hospital in Nguiu.

John Kelantumama, Nguiu policeman.

Jimmy Tipungwuti, Chairman of the Tiwi Land
Council.

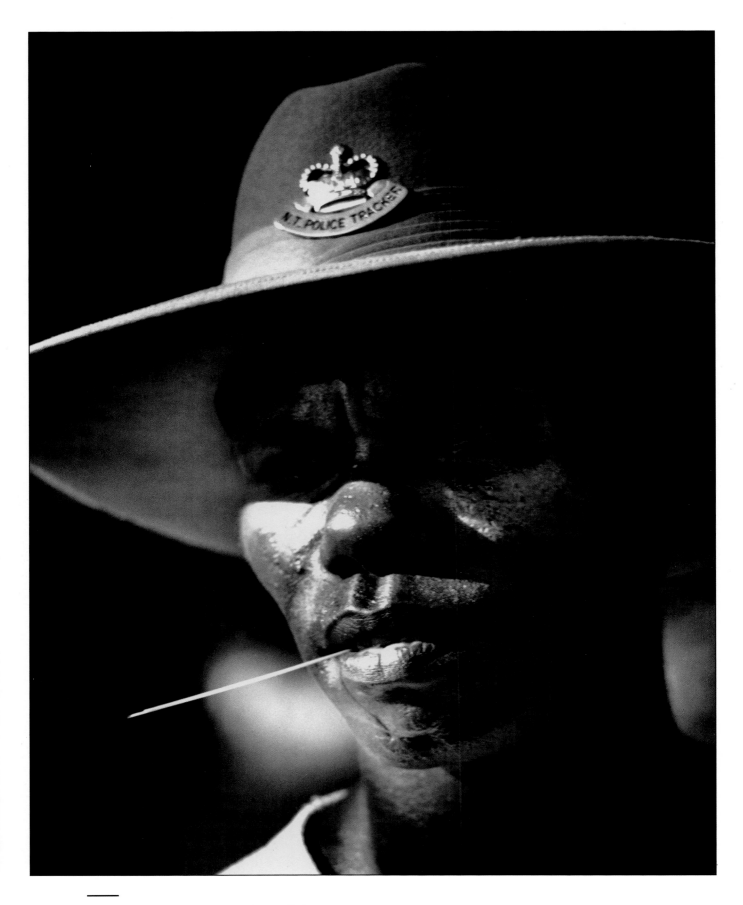

Regis Pangarimini, police tracker at Pularumpi.

Blanche Puruntatameri, Bathurst Island.

Dorothy Tipungwuti at her (now cyclone-proof) home.

Tiwi girls grow up fast—Sarah Kerinaiua, her sister
Francina and Mona Lisa Kantilla are still in their
teens.

Young family of Snake Bay. Ray Bush, his wife
Enunciata and son Gerard.

Mark Mungatopi with his pig, also called
Mungatopi. Mark described his pig as 'cheeky',
which means it's best to keep out of its way.

Paddy Henry Ripijingimpi and his wife Nancy,
cooking breakfast at Milikapiti.

Paul Wilson and Sharon Heenan-Tipungwuti,
Milikapiti.

Amos Tungatalum with his father Leonard.

The late Raphael Apuatimi, another of the founders
of Tiwi Design.

The late Thomas Woody of Pularumpi.

Marjorie Wonamirri, Marie Porkalari and Topsy
Kerinaiua, three widows from Paru going bush to
find tucker.

A quick douse with a mug of water brings temporary
relief from the heat.

Even the camp dogs feel the heat during the Wet.

Edith Munkara at the entrance to her traditional
bush shelter. These shelters have a framework of
forked sticks and are covered with paperbark and
pandanus palm leaves.

Bush camps have changed a bit—this one has a
tent. The campsite is near a freshwater stream with
plenty of shade.

When the village is deserted in the dry season,
the priest also goes bush to conduct Mass.

Sunset is a favourite playtime for children and dogs.

The fish traps near Nguiu are also a hunting
place for sea eagles and crocodiles.

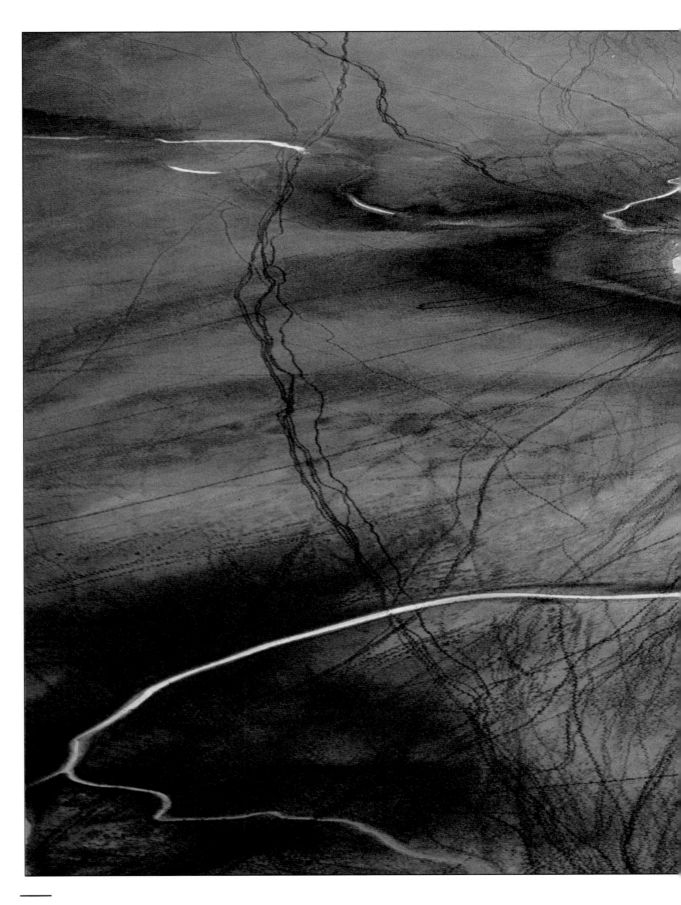

Buffalo tracks crisscross the wetlands on Melville
Island. Plans to domesticate these animals are
hampered by the fact that the wetlands are almost
inaccessible.

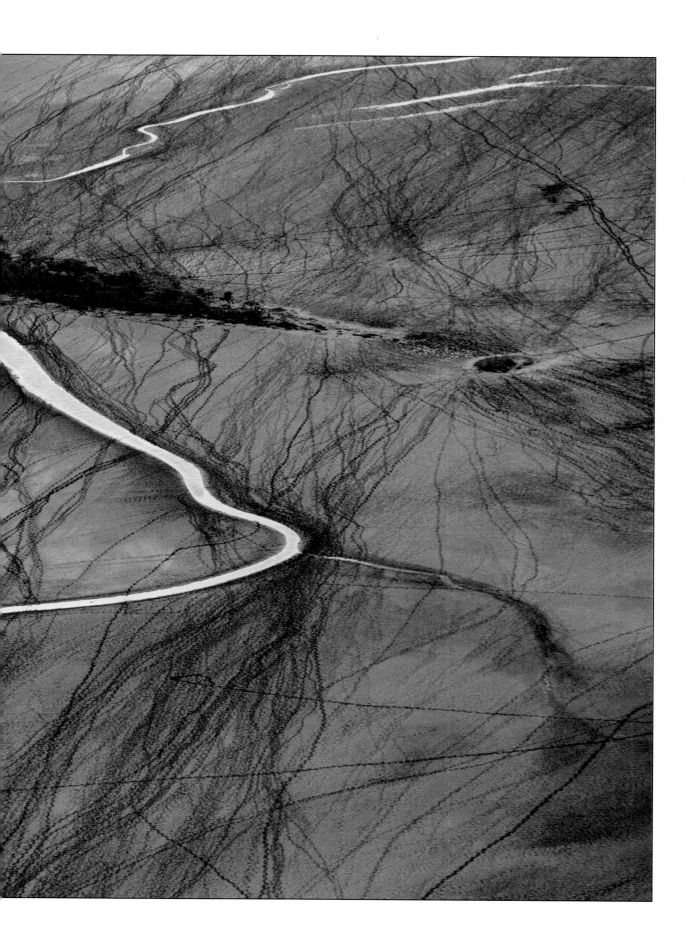

Ethelita Bading chewing on a sweet-tasting palm root.

The yuwurli, or mangrove worm, is perhaps the
most prized item on the menu for the Tiwi. It is
regarded as both a delicacy and a 'pick-me-up'.

The bucket holds a feast of mud crabs.

Gerardine is using the lid of her billy to reflect
light into a dead tree to look for yilinga, or copper
snake.

Above: Valma is searching for sugarbag, which is
the name for the native bee and also the name
for the honey. Below: Here she looks for possums
in the trees.

Afternoon tea after a day on the beach—turtle eggs
and a cuppa.

The wallaby has been hanging in a tree to dry.
This way the family uses only as much as is needed
for one meal.

Small fish are caught with a net in the shallow
waters.

Crab hunting, traditionally done by women and children, is always an adventure. A stick or two is used to hold the crab down and the claws are handled with old rags.

Heading home with the catch.

The crab is thrown straight onto the campfire; the
salt water provides the seasoning.

Tiwi boys are extremely accurate with their sling
shots. Fortunately the weapon is mainly used to
knock mangos out of trees.

Boys sitting amongst the pandanus nuts
(wurranya), which are only edible when they turn
brown.

A lot of fun with a tantalising element of danger:
the drop to the pool is about fifteen metres.

A perfect place to spend the school holidays.

A super-size cowrie shell.

In the mangroves.

Practising future hunting techniques.

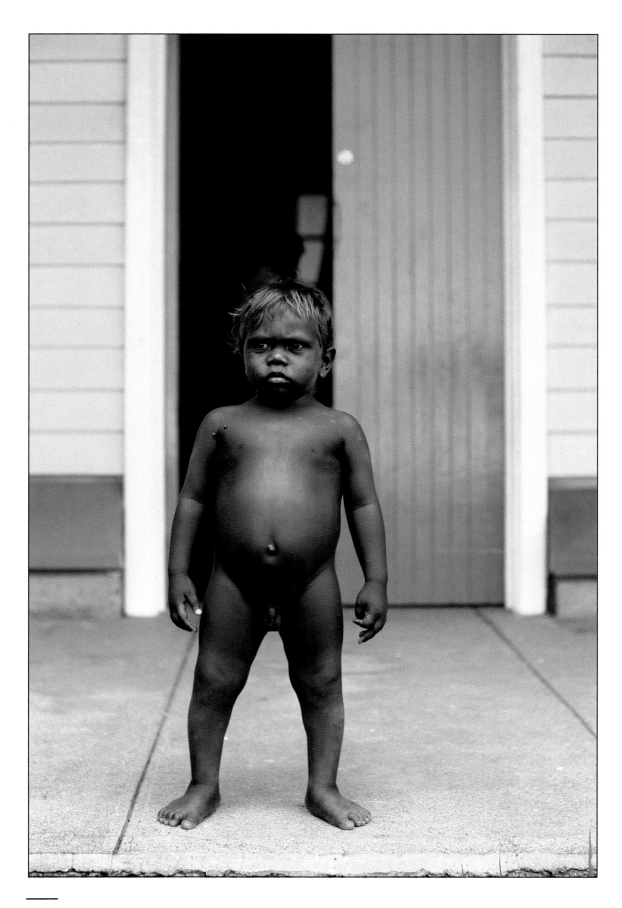

Elija, waiting outside the doctor's surgery for his
checkup. The health workers keep a very close eye
on infants and young children.

Children often spend all day on the beach.

Tony Apuatimi, silhouetted in the sunset.

Catching the last of the sun's rays on the beach
at Port Hurd.

He's not really camera shy, he just needs a little
gentle persuasion.

It's easy to make your own entertainment in this natural playground.

The slightly older children look after the young
ones. A Tiwi child takes on responsibilities at an
early age.

A fringe benefit from the new world outside—the
iceblock.

Samuela, trying on the concept of fashion.

Smiles come without coaxing from these
youngsters.

Xavier Poantumilui: warrior or fisherman?

Tiwi children begin to learn the crafts of carving
and painting at an early age.

Team photo.

Eusebia Puantulura coming home from school.
There is water everywhere during the wet and the
children love it.

Playing in the wet.

Sharlene Heenan-Tipungwuti.

Leonita Kerinaiua.

Tiwi or penguin?

Waiting for the next wave.

Casual but stylish at the beach.

Lisa Grace Moreen Mungatopi gnawing on a crab
leg.

Child in the lush surrounds of the rainforest.

Playing in the creek bed.